In Opening the Gate to New Worlds: How to Write a Book Children Will Treasure

Lauren Bingham

Contents

Introduction

Do you remember the first book that ever made an impression on you as a child? The one that opened your eyes to a whole new worldview, or awoke your imagination to wild new adventures?

What do you remember about that book? Do you still quote your favorite passages? Can you remember the pictures you loved the most? You might even remember how the book felt in your hands and the smell of the pages, or poring over the pages in your favorite childhood reading spot. Many of us recall hiding under the blankets with a flashlight, skipping a full night of sleep in favor of finding a good stopping point in a great book, despite being up way past our bedtimes. In fact, I think I might still be grounded for staying up all night once in fifth grade when the copy of Roald Dahl's *Matilda* my friends were passing around made it into my hands.

For many of us, reading was just as good as–if not better than—television. We could escape to places far away, meet historical figures, and learn about the world around us, all while snuggled up in a safe place where we could focus on our reading.

As a child, I wanted nothing more than to be a writer. I wanted to tell the stories that mattered to people. My childhood was spent surrounded by books that changed my life: from *Goodnight Moon* by Margaret Wise Brown, to *Misty of Chincoteague* by Marguerite Henry, to every *Nancy Drew* book written between the inception of the series and 1994, when I entered high school literature classes and had to devote almost all of my reading time to classics for upcoming essays.

But even as I wrapped my teenage brain around Camus, Dostoevsky, and Dumas, I eagerly looked for an opportunity to bond with a book as deeply as I had in my earliest years of reading. And while there have been hundreds of books that have had lasting impact on my life, when I'm asked what my favorite book of all time is, I come back to my childhood favorites. The books I read on the sofa, in the car, under the covers—even recently. In times when others might turn to binge-watching a familiar show, I find myself crawling between the pages of *The Phantom Tollbooth*. Milo's journey towards the Kingdom of Wisdom, as skillfully detailed by author Norton Juster, has always been awfully similar to the challenges I've encountered in my life. Milo's terror in the face of change, adversity, and confusion is so familiar that even a teenage version of myself would find sound advice in the poor boy's adventures.

But you're not reading this to get a list of my favorite childhood books—though I could happily prattle on for many pages about all of the books that have changed my life. You're here because you would like to write a book for children. As such, we're going to spend the next several chapters discussing what makes a good children's book, from the topic you choose to the words you use and the way you connect with your audience.

We all have different reasons for wanting to write a book for children. Perhaps, like me, you have a profound connection to some of the books from your childhood. Maybe you have a very special story to tell that you wish someone had shared with you when you were younger. You might want to give young people more information about the world around them, or you might want to create a brand-new world where they can let their imaginations soar.

Whatever your reason for wanting to write a book specifically for children, I commend it. I'm also very impressed that you've chosen to pick up this book. That tells me that you're committed to the task and want to do your very best for young readers. I also recognize that you might be feeling a little less than 100% confident in this endeavor; otherwise, you probably wouldn't pick up a book with "How to" in the title.

As I've shared in my other books, confidence and having the gumption to keep writing, even when you feel like you're not doing your very best, is a large part of the writing process. Above all, the most important advice I can share is to start writing and continue writing, even when your mind is telling you it's not worth the effort. It's always worth the effort, and regardless of whether you achieve best-seller status or not, the personal satisfaction of seeing your words in print never gets old.

But, as with every type of writing, there are nuances that aspiring authors should keep in mind when writing for children. The most significant of these is that your audience is, in fact, children.

This may seem a foregone conclusion, but as someone who has dabbled in children's books many times over the years, I have to admit that it can be easy to forget what it's like to be a child.

Children don't think like adults and thank goodness for that. Children process topics differently than we do. They have a wildly different worldview from adults, with less experience in processing the agonies of life, and a much greater likelihood of being enthralled with life's ecstasies. Everything is new to children, from experiencing cultures and learning about events for the first time to developing their vocabulary. Even the emotions children experience are unfamiliar to them.

Of course, these are just a few of the things writers like you and I must consider when composing a book for children. There are the same quandaries authors have faced since the beginning of time, like how to choose a topic, how much detail to include, what angle to take towards the topic at hand. But you have to deal with a few extras, like whether you should include pictures or a glossary to help your young readers grow more familiar with the topic. You not only have to understand who your audience is, but what they're capable of understanding. You have to decide how much to challenge their current knowledge while maintaining a comfortable, accessible tone. You aren't just a writer—you're a teacher and a guide through an unfamiliar world.

Whether or not you want or intend to write a deeply meaningful book for children, your readers may see things a little differently. Each new page turned, each picture seen for the first time, and every new word added to their vocabulary is a completely fresh experience for young readers. You don't necessarily have to try to make an impression on youngsters—sometimes you just do.

Writing for children comes a bit more naturally for some than others. My personal weakness is vocabulary. I subconsciously expect every child to have the same affinity for new words I did as a youngster, but that's simply not realistic. Thankfully, I have a pool of young nieces and nephews I can test my wording on, and who can also help me understand what kids are into these days.

So, whether you're an out-of-touch Auntie like I am or a childcare or educational professional who speaks fluent Preschooler, there are parts of this book that may seem obvious to you, while others may be major revelations. My goal here is to encourage each future children's book author to consider each of the moving parts that go into the writing process. Furthermore, you'll get the opportunity to put it all together for yourself with a few practice exercises scattered throughout the book.

As always, I encourage you to have your writing supplies handy as you read along. I find that inspiration doesn't always strike when you're face-to-face with your draft, but keeping a notebook (digital or paper) nearby can definitely help capture some of those "aha!" moments.

Whether you're not quite ready to start your first chapter or looking for a final wizened perspective to help you fine-tune your first children's book before you send it to publishers, I hope this book is a starting place for a pleasantly memorable journey through the world of writing for the younger reader. We all have important voices, and the stories we share with the younger generation truly have an impact on our future.

First Things First: What Is a Kid's Book?

I chose to make this its own major section in the book because it's very important, and you'll want to be able to find it again easily.

Writing books for children is especially nuanced because our audience is in the process of learning to read. Despite popular rumors, even I didn't come out of the womb reading chapter books.

Therefore, the most important thing we need to keep in mind when writing a children's book is the age group or reading level we're hoping will read the book.

It's surprisingly difficult to find experts who agree on kids' reading levels. This makes sense since all children are on their own individual learning pathways. The differences between what is taught in schools can also vary wildly. My fifth-grade vocabulary book and my ninth-grade vocabulary book were different editions of the same book— I remember the odd sense of deja vu I felt when I realized the smiling cartoon children waving from the cover of the book were the exact same children I'd encountered four years earlier. I had simply transferred to a school district where the language arts program wasn't as robust.

With that in mind, please take this list as somewhat of a general guide/discussion regarding age groups, grades, and reading levels:

Ages 2-5 : Early Picture Books

"Early" picture books refer to books that have large format pictures and few words. Typically, they tell less of a story than they describe or label things so that children can match the word with a picture of the object.

My old favorite *Goodnight Moon* comes to mind here. It's less of a story than a process of the narrator saying "goodnight" to their surroundings. But even decades later, I remember my father pointing to the words. "Do you see a mouse in the picture? A mouse?" He would point to the word so I could see what "mouse" looked like in letters. The Berenstain Bears (mysteriously known to GenX and Millennials as "The Berenstein Bears") are another example of early picture books that can advance with children through this entire age group, with simple lessons and bright, understandable pictures.

At this stage in their lives, children don't really have the ability to process complex pictures, words, or ideas. They're aware of the moon as a bright object in the night sky, for example, but they aren't quite ready to accept that it's an enormous rocky satellite that's bound to the Earth by gravitational forces. They have absolutely no questions about how Brother Bear and Sister Bear get into some of their wacky pratfalls, but everyone learns a lesson and everything turns out ok.

Ultimately, these books are designed to be read to children to help them become familiar with words and letters as well as all the concepts they're experiencing for the first time. Getting ready for bed, using manners, and making good choices don't come naturally—ask any-body with a toddler!

Children may not be reading all of the words themselves, so it's a good idea for books at this age level to be somewhat interactive. For example, an adult might ask questions as they read with the child, such as "What is the person in this drawing doing?" or "What do you think will happen next?"

Book length is an important factor here, as well. Getting through an entire plot arc before the young one is bored, hungry, or has to go to the potty requires a fine touch for authors in this age group.

Ages 5-8 : Picture Books, Coloring and Activity Books, Novelty Books

"Early" picture books and regular picture books really only differ in their complexity. Picture books for this age group have an entire sentence or two accompanying each picture. The pictures may depict full activities instead of simple concepts, and use more colors and details.

Consider a book about autumn activities. An early picture book may present a simple fact, like "Dot has an apple", accompanied by a picture of a person holding a bright red apple.

The picture book version of this may be more along the lines of "Dot and Johnny are going apple picking. They picked red apples and green apples." The picture would then show two people and apple trees, some of them with red apples and others with green fruit dangling from the branches.

While early picture books address a single concept, a picture book for this age group tells a complete story. It shouldn't be a long story, of course, but picture books for more experienced readers can have a beginning, a climax, and an end. It's a good idea to stick to one plot line at a time, as well. *The Polar Express* or *Jumanji* by Chris Van Allsburg are examples of picture books that appeal to audiences of all ages, with detailed artwork and mysterious-yet-somehow-relatable plotlines.

Coloring and activity books are more fun ways to engage youngsters in matching words and pictures. The interaction with adding color to a scene, unscrambling words, or doing a seek-and-find can help new readers connect objects and concepts with the words they read.

The first thing that comes to mind when I think of "novelty books" are the little paper books restaurants used to give kids to keep them occupied while waiting for food, but that shows my age. Those books have long since been converted to paper placemats. However, you'll still find the occasional small-format short story tucked in kids' meals or at events like weddings where children might need a little extra entertainment. I once worked on a family history that was presented like a storybook for the younger generations attending a massive family reunion, and the concept was admirable and adorable.

Ultimately, books in this age range are designed to gently push readers to add a few more words to their vocabulary, a few more minutes to their reading time, and a few more questions to their mind. (Sorry, parents!)

Ages 4-9 : Early/Easy Readers

This is a tricky group to write for, simply because this is the heart of the time when children are typically doing the most learning.

In many American school districts, children start school with kindergarten at age 5. Most schools request that students recognize their alphabet before they start school, but this is not always the case. At the same time, I also recognize that there are daycares and preschools that operate on an accelerated learning schedule and can provide a more acute analysis of *Pete the Cat* than I can.

Appropriate books for this age group are typically longer than the average picture book. There may be entire pages that do not have pictures, and readers may be tasked with entire paragraphs of text to read. The topics may get a little more complex, and there may be more than just a handful of characters for the reader to keep track of.

As you can imagine, this is where reading can get tricky for some kids. Without the benefit of large print and many pictures, they are challenged to use more of their knowledge and understanding. And, since there is no linear process for experiencing how the world works, a book that is perfect for one reader may be wildly inappropriate for another. At this reading level, it's often a good idea for adults to help children pick their books to ensure there are no unpleasant surprises.

Non-fiction writers take note: this is the stage at which children start gaining a voracious appetite for favorite topics. Some children have a certain tenacity in learning, in which they'll fixate on a particular topic and do their best to attain expert status through whatever resources they can get their hands on. As a writer, I like to assume that readers in this age group are going to read whatever they can get their hands on regarding the topic I choose, which means I need to be able to provide new and interesting information to satisfy them.

On a similar note to fiction writers, many children discover their favorite genres at this reading level. Historical fiction, fantasy, science-fiction, and even light mysteries can be part of the literary experience, though in a much briefer and less intense version than their adult counterparts. Consider, for example, Robert Munsch's *Paper Bag Princess*, which has started many a young reader on a love of fantasy books. Or maybe, like me, you loved reading and learning more about the real lives of the people discussed in history class– early reader biographies beget young history buffs.

Ages 6-10 : Beginner Chapter Books, Early Non-Fiction

If you look carefully at the age group, you'll notice that this range can encompass students in Kindergarten through fifth grade, depending on their learning path. As noted earlier, individual readers will likely have different levels of understanding, vocabulary, and interest in certain topics.

As a result, beginner chapter books tend to be a little more niche than other types of young reader literature. The *Junie B. Jones* series, for example, follows an "almost six-year-old" as she follows clues and hunches to find solutions for the mysterious problems that come her way. The hook for these books is the excitement of a mystery accompanied by a character that speaks and acts the way an almost six-year-old would.

Beginner chapter books may also expand on a familiar story, like the plot of a movie or television show. My favorite example here is the *Star Wars* franchise. Readers of any level or age group can find books geared towards them. The readers' familiarity with the content and characters can help guide them through seeing that same plot unfold in a book, giving them an extra level of context to the words as they read them.

Children are a mystery at this stage, craving an outlet for their imaginations and thirsting for more knowledge in equal parts. Children's play at age 10 evolves significantly from their play at age 6, with storylines and topics becoming more realistic and complicated. Frequently, kids in this group will latch onto particular characters or scenarios—this was when I experienced peak consumption of early-1930s *Nancy Drew* books, for example.

The best—and worst!—thing about writing beginning chapter books is that if a child were to read that book each year between ages 6 and 10, they would experience that book in an entirely different way each time. There are so many changes in this timeframe—mentally, physically, emotionally, and educationally—that re-reading these early books can bring a new understanding each time. This is a wonderful thing for you as a writer, as long as your audience encounters your life-changing book at the right time in this period of growth. It can also be heartbreaking to see a reader miss that window in which that book could have had its greatest impact. You'll know these readers by their use of phrases like "I wish I had read this book as a kid" and the personal anguish you feel when they tell you why.

You've probably noticed that I've added "early non-fiction" to this age group, as well. This is the age group where fiction and non-fiction truly diverge. While the actual text and topic of books from earlier reading levels may be solidly classified as "fiction" or "non-fiction," the format in which the text and topic are presented is quite similar. Readers are given pictures and large print words to help them piece together information about the subject of the book, whether that's learning about different types of bugs or finding out where Harold is headed with his purple crayon.

In the 6-10 age group, many children are ready for short books with more text than pictures. Generally, these books are not super-detailed and provide a quick, factual overview of a topic. Early non-fiction books may have a few chapters and answer very specific questions that might be common for readers at that age. Think of topics like "Who Was Babe Ruth?" "How Do Hummingbirds Fly?" or "What Happened to the Titanic?" Historical, scientific, and biographical nonfiction topics are popular among this age group as they supplement knowledge imparted to them in school.

Still, there are some among this age group who are still unconvinced that reading a single book dedicated to a topic can be an easier option than conducting a dozen semi-fruitful Google searches. In fact, I know quite a few adults with the same thought process, so perhaps I should say that this predilection starts in this age group.

Ages 8-12 : Middle-Grade Novels, Non-Fiction

Middle-grade novels are lots of fun for writers because we have the opportunity to explore a greater variety of topics and introduce a far more imaginative array of characters, concepts, and plot lines.

That being said, children in this age group are often under immense pressure to do things besides reading for fun. They not only have plenty of schoolwork to do but they might be involved in extracurricular activities like sports, theatre, or band. They likely have chores to complete, video games to conquer, and an increasingly complicated social network to navigate.

That is to say that when you are writing for these kids, you're competing with a million other stimuli in their young lives. You may have very little time to really capture their attention and make them want to dedicate their precious time to your pages.

At the same time, readers in the 8-12 group are still very much children. They throw themselves into playing and using their imagination. They are absorbing information from every facet of their lives at such an astounding rate that they don't even realize they're learning. This is the peak time for engaging their minds in the world of reading.

There are quite a few theories on how to deal with this phenomenon. Online content writers believe that putting a keyword in each sentence and keeping paragraphs to fewer than three lines of print will keep the attention of a stressed and hard-pressed reader. Fiction writers often try to come up with brilliant, innovative plots and deeply sympathetic emotional situations that readers find attractive.

But what about the poor non-fiction writers? Are they doomed to only write research material for this age group?

Yes and no. Yes, because anything can be used as research material if it provides you with new facts. No, because it is possible to capture the attention of a curious pre-teen and maybe even satiate their curiosity. Kids have a lot of questions at this age, and sometimes they learn that asking questions is inappropriate, or that asking questions is a sign of weakness. I don't know exactly when stifling children's growth became a social norm in the Western world, but I do know that many of my childhood questions were answered factually and appropriately through books. We can't always trust the internet to be factual or appropriate, so I am pleased to know that many parents are looking toward self-help, health, psychology, and philosophical books for children in this age group who have questions or are processing heavy situations.

So, while it might seem hard to get the attention of this age group, it's important to note that they may be some of the most loyal and devoted young readers. Kids of this age have the emotional understanding to connect with characters on a more personal level, plus, many of them have been impacted by harsh, stressful situations. Divorce, death, moving, new siblings, friend group drama, and disabilities are topics that can cause great upheaval for kids in this age group, and finding characters or content that comforts them can be immensely helpful in healing. Recurring characters and book series are often very popular in this age group, so be prepared to keep up with the demand if you go that route!

Ages 12-18 : Young Adult (YA) Novels, Non-Fiction

As a member of GenX, this is about the age at which I was introduced to Stephen King's short stories. And yes, I understood every word—I had a dictionary and an encyclopedia, thank you very much.

That being said, I'd like to think that parents today have learned what *IT*-induced nightmares can do for youthful well-being, and are steering their children towards more appropriate books for their age group.

Both the words in the term "Young Adult" are accurate here. For the most part, readers in this group will be going through or have gone through puberty. They will probably have seen some PG-13 movies, which include things like guns, smoking, language, and sexual implications. They have likely been exposed to true crime investigation shows on television and have gathered a collection of naughty words and concepts through their peers that would make George Carlin's "7 Words" look as scandalous as a grocery list. I say this not to upset any parents who might be reading this, but whether or not your child is engaging in any of this activity or material, it is pretty common to encounter this kind of content at a high school.

At the same time, ages 12-17 are legally children, and there are plenty of adult books out there that deal with adult topics in adult ways. YA books are ideal for teenagers who prefer to read about characters in their own age group and do things that relate to their lives—such as going to school, going steady for the first time, having friend group spats, and preparing for college.

Another thing to keep in mind is that the Young Adult crowd has well-established their favorite genre. While they may tolerate a little romance in their fantasy book, for example, they're generally here for either one or the other. They may prefer books with certain tropes, like forbidden love, secrets, or forced proximity. They may look for characters like the anti-hero, the mentor, or the bumbling everyman.

If we stop and think about it for a moment, teen readers tend to gravitate towards certain topics. Consider Suzanne Collins' *Hunger Games* trilogy, the *Twilight* series, or anything Harry Potter-adjacent. Being a teenager is a confusing, tumultuous time in life. Characters and situations in which these characters are feeling awkward, out of place, or even threatened are relatable for so many of the readers in this group. Though they aren't actually being hunted for sport like Katniss Everdeen, the pressures of their daily lives– school, social life, sports, activities, jobs, and the looming pressure of getting into this mysterious thing called "college"- can make it feel like making a single wrong turn will ultimately lead to their immediate doom.

This is an age group in which many young people feel disconnected—like no one understands them or what they're going through. A lot of Young Adult series feature characters who echo these feelings and fears, but non-fiction has a huge role in providing solace to this age group, as well. Self-help and philosophical books for teenagers can help them understand, appreciate, and manage the myriad emotions and thoughts that are coursing through their minds each day.

Interestingly enough, biographies, autobiographies, and memoirs can be especially influential for readers in this age group. Young adults tend to look for adults to serve as mentors who can guide them through the extraordinarily confusing years of early adulthood. Understanding the trials and tribulations of some of their heroes or popular public figures can be inspiring and even deter teen readers from making some of the same mistakes.

I would like to reiterate that these are only generalized age and reading groups. I personally feel that picture books are appropriate for all ages. I will always care about *Pat the Bunny*, but reading *Midnight Hour Encores* by Bruce Brooks was a huge moment for me as an adolescent. They both have places of honor on my bookshelves.

The Young Adult segment is so expansive and growing at such an amazing rate that it would take me an entire book to explain the ins and outs of targeting this audience. This is actually one of my own personal audiences to write for because of how far you can go with a YA reader's imagination. Even though they may proclaim things as "lame" or whatever vernacular indicates uncoolness, they are still quite willing to fire up the old make-believe processor in the brain—when provided with appropriate ignition. And that's why writing for this group is so complicated. Consider this an introductory lesson and look for a more thorough lesson in the future.

As we wrap up this review of potential reading levels, I'd also like to point out that there's a lot of flexibility between the stages, as well. There are also no hard and fast rules that state that a teenager is forbidden from enjoying a picture book.

At the end of the day, only the reader, their caregiver, and their educational team can really assess whether or not your book is appropriate for that particular individual. As a writer, you have to accept that not all readers within an age group will appreciate your material in the same way. If you release your material to the public, you will likely receive equal amounts of feedback that your book is "too old" or "too young" for the intended audience. All of them are likely accurate, but that's not your fault.

It can be somewhat intimidating to sit back and watch readers and parents bicker over whether your book is appropriate for the advertised age group. Please do not let this prevent you from writing a book for children. I know this sounds like ridiculous advice, along the lines of "Yes, the dog bites, but go ahead and pet him"—but hear me out.

Unless your book is wildly inappropriate for children altogether, a book that contains vocabulary and topics that are above or below a child's learning level shouldn't cause trauma for the reader or the writer. It might inconvenience them, or bore them, or fail to connect with them, but whether the reader chooses to use that as a stopping point or a learning opportunity is up to the individual.

That being said, there are several things you as the author can do to ensure that readers of your intended age group are getting exactly what they expect. From a clear description to sharing text samples that truly exemplify the contents of your book, there are ways to set expectations with your readers before they even open the book.

Even more importantly—and the reason for this book—there are ways you can meet and exceed readers' expectations once they do open the book.

Now that we have a clearer understanding of the different age and reading groups and the material they'll be interested in reading, let's look deeper into the traits and techniques children's book authors can employ to help them craft the perfect book for their readers.

Chapter One

Building a Book for Children

I could have said "writing" or "crafting" a book for children, but for me, the process really feels like building. You have to carefully construct a plot, then strategically fill it with characters while being ever-so-delicate with the words you use. For me, building a project like this requires a blueprint, or at least a very good plan.

Your Children's Book Blueprint

As I've mentioned in my other books, your version of an outline or blueprint may be very different from mine. In fact, my own outline changes form several times through the writing of a book. For the sake of this "How To" book, I'll share examples of my basic forms and formatting so that you may appreciate the basic concept and adapt it to your own brain flow. So, if you're reading along and thinking "I would never do that!" please know that I understand and encourage you to think of how you would do it instead. I'm just the guide in this book—your actual writing experience is your own!

It's entirely ok if you want to flip my process upside down. Take a look at the chapter headings and decide where your own questions lead you. I promise I won't be offended. I encourage you to use this resource as inspiration for your own personal flow, rather than a strict code of conduct when building a book.

My own personal blueprint starts by answering the most basic questions:

- What am I building?

- Who is going to use it?

- How should I build it?

Initially, the answers to these questions will be pretty basic, too:

- A book for children

- Children who can read simple chapter books

- Typing 15,000 words seems like a good start

But every idea begins with just the most basic concepts, doesn't it? Rome wasn't built in a day, and *Gone with the Wind* wasn't jotted down in a single sitting. Don't be afraid to make notes that feel redundant or obvious, because, at some point in the future, those notes may be your lifeline back to your original project idea. Blueprints frequently change, after all.

Let's get back to the very first question, though: What are you building?

Choosing the topic you write about or the reading level you're writing for is a bit of a "chicken and the egg"- type argument. You may find yourself hopelessly compelled to write a book to help children learn about a certain person, place, or event—real or imagined. Maybe some of your imaginary games as a child had a pretty good plot, and you'd like to capture the adventures you dreamt up in words before they disappear.

Alternatively, you might have a particular child or group of children in mind when you start your book. When my friend's daughter was very young, I used to love writing simple little illustrated stories on the backs of paper restaurant menus while we waited for our supper to arrive. The protagonist of these stories was always my friend's daughter, and the story was always exceptionally relevant to whatever was new in her young world.

Topic and reading level do somewhat go hand-in-hand. An early picture book about a serious topic like the Civil War would be challenging, but an early chapter book is quite feasible, as evidenced by the Addie Walker stories in the American Girl book series. At the same time, an early picture book about a cardboard box could be wildly successful, while a YA book would struggle with a topic so simple.

For the sake of this being a text-based book that requires organization, I've decided to start with the process of choosing a topic, but fear not—selecting the appropriate age and reading group is not far behind. You can read them in reverse order if you like—please feel free to make this book a guide that gives you the most insight into your writing process, even if that means jumping around a bit!

One of the easiest ways to stop the inspiration from flowing—full stop, not even a drizzle of thought—is to try to do something in a way that doesn't make sense to you. Sometimes we need to force things a little bit to get the literary stream moving again, sort of like pushing rocks and debris out of an actual body of water stream to prevent it from creating a dam. That sort of thing can actually be pretty helpful in allowing you to discover why you have so much rubbish accumulated in your literary stream.

But trying to keep an already functioning stream going with some-one else's cleaning equipment can be tricky. As such, I always en-courage my readers to read along and try some of my suggestions and exercises, but if they aren't really inspiring you—go ahead and make them your own! If you've got a problem, and someone hands you a tool, use it in a way that solves the problem, not in the way you think it has to be used.

On that note, we'll start exploring how to build the foundation for a children's book you'll be proud of.

Become An Agent of Discovery

There's a lot of pressure on writers to create a book that isn't too basic but isn't too complicated, either. This isn't exclusive to children's writers, either—plenty of adults want that "just right" spot of having enough plot twists or information without becoming too confusing or overbearing. Fiction or nonfiction, it is very hard to hit every single reader's Goldilocks spot of perfection when it comes to creating a book.

When it comes to writing for children, you have to walk into each word and each page with the understanding that your reader has probably never heard of this topic or read these words in this order before this very moment. Everything is new, and it needs to be presented in a more simplistic way.

At the same time, you are likely aware that children frequently have an unquenchable thirst for knowledge with an unending series of "Why?" I admire that quality in children, but I also acknowledge that answering questions like "Why did people think they could own other people as slaves?" or "Why doesn't my best friend's mom love her husband anymore?" is difficult, troubling, and often emotional for adults.

As a children's author, I encourage you to think of yourself as an agent of discovery. The information that you publish—written, diagram, illustration, photograph, whatever form it takes—is going to open some child's eyes to a new understanding of something.

Not all of these discoveries are poignant. Sometimes the new understanding is low-emotion, like the moment you learn that b-a-l-l-o-o-n spells the name of that inflated thing floating on a string in the drawing above the word.

Other times, the new information gleaned from this work of literature will be somewhat life-altering. I think a lot of young readers are changed by books like *Tuck Everlasting*, *Bridge to Terabithia*, or *Where the Red Fern Grows*. I was absolutely devastated by books like *The Velveteen Rabbit* and *Charlotte's Web*, myself.

However, sooner or later children are going to experience situations like those depicted in these books. Whether they have lost a pet, a friend, or a dream, bad things happen to people of all ages. As writers, we shouldn't necessarily avoid heavy topics like life and death—we just want to make sure we deliver this information in a way that readers of a younger age can connect to appropriately.

You might be surprised by what does and doesn't upset some children. When discussing the topic of divorce in a book I wrote years ago, some of the editors were concerned that it was too heavy a topic for early chapter book readers. That is, until we received a review from a child who explained to us that divorce isn't always sad. In fact, this particular reader's mummy was much happier now that she'd left Daddy and found Mark. We thanked that reader for their personal insight and congratulated their mother on her newfound bliss, and learned the importance of keeping our minds open that day.

Building the Book for the Reader

Ultimately, choosing the perfect topic requires a little hands-on research. I'm not saying "Go find a child and talk to them about life-and-death level topics," but if you are a parent, caregiver, family member, or friend to a child in the age group you're gearing your book towards, you might take the opportunity to talk to them about your topic—in a way that is appropriate for them. Perhaps you discuss a movie or book that has a similar topic. Maybe you bring up current events in that child's life in a sensitive way. Don't go out of your way to traumatize anyone, but if you want to know how much a 6-year-old suburban girl understands about American colonization and its impact on native peoples, it's a good idea to go directly to the source.

For those who do not have access to a plethora of children for a test panel, fear not - the internet exists. While each teacher has their own admirable lesson plan and materials available, teachers use the same internet that you and I do. You can search for handouts, activity pages, talking points, and lesson guides for loads of topics for nearly every age group.

Benefits of doing this extra bit of research include:

1. **Additional insight into the keywords and concepts that are popularly shared with children in this age group.** By reading what children are reading, you'll appreciate the type of introduction children are getting to your chosen topic.

Be sure to pay attention to the vocabulary and sentence structure these materials use—that will give you an idea of what your audience is familiar with. Sometimes a topic is hard to approach not because children don't have the ability to understand the content, but the words and processes involved.

An example that comes to mind is astrophysics. Children have the ability to understand that things like planets, moons, suns, and galaxies exist. They can piece together how big each of these things is, and even conceptualize the enormity of space compared to the size of something more familiar, like Earth.

However, if you start asking children to measure the potential organic compounds of distant planets based solely on spectrometry, a lot of kiddos might struggle. First, it's going to be hard for the under-18 crowd to get their hands on a spectrograph or spectrometer. Then there's a lot of math involved, which makes the topic much better for someone other than children. Or me.

Researching your topic through the lens of a child will help you get on their level for presenting new information to them. While many children surely will eventually develop a love for solar-induced chlorophyll fluorescence and leaf pulses, they first need to understand leaves and photosynthesis.

Knowing what words and concepts can be adequately explained and described to children while simultaneously piquing their interest is a huge help for me when really narrowing down my children's book topic. While I'm a major proponent of writing books that require kids to look up a word or term here and there, a book that presents entirely new topic material without context or a solid foundation for learning will not be popular with your intended audience. The goal is to challenge readers, not force them to skip a grade or two in order to get through your book.

2. Getting insight into who your narrator/point of view might be. Whether you are writing fiction or nonfiction, you'll need to decide on a point of view from which your information is delivered.

First-person (I/me) and third-person (he/she/they) are pretty common delivery methods for fictional pieces. Second-person (you) is not as common in children's works, but I have seen it used quite successfully in non-fiction style books that allow readers to feel like they're "discovering" a topic through words and pictures.

Picture books tend to use an omniscient point of view—that is, the information is shared by someone who knows everything all at once. The trick is to be able to have an omniscient narrator concentrate exclusively on the story to avoid overwhelming a young audience.

The Very Hungry Caterpillar, for example, uses an omniscient narrator who follows the main character caterpillar through the very particular process of eating and growing. Author Eric Carle could have certainly gone into greater detail about how caterpillars and butterflies work, but instead, he laser-focused the plot on a larval insect hoping to satisfy his hunger. However, in doing so, he created a book that helps children with counting skills, learning the days of the week, and understanding that there are good and not-so-good food choices.

The point of view character or narrator is not just the motivation for storytelling in a children's book. In a world in which we consider every word has the ability to teach the reader something new, the narrator becomes a guide, teacher, and discussion leader. As you research books related to your topic, think very hard about who that teacher is going to be.

Even in non-fiction books, the point of view matters. Facts are wonderful, but they have to be presented in a way that is sympathetic to the young reader's experience. That is, the data you provide has to be presented in a way that readers want to learn more about it. Take, for example, Joanna Cole's *The Magic School Bus* book series. I distinctly remember my sixth-grade science teacher showing us diagrams of the human digestive tract, but I learned far more when Ms. Frizzle shrank the bus down to drive through it.

We'll talk more about character development within the confines of a children's book in a later chapter, but at this stage of creating your topic, it's a good idea to actively think about how you're going to present this topic from every angle.

3. The opportunity to familiarize yourself with the market.
As you read the types of things children are already reading about your topic, you can get a feel for what kind of questions, thoughts, and emotions your readers will expect from that topic.

Additionally, this will allow you to have the same knowledge base as your audience, thus allowing you to throw in extra information or a new angle that differentiates your book from everything else in its niche.

Writing a book that children will enjoy assumes a certain amount of familiarity or curiosity regarding the topic. As a result, many authors will focus their writing on what they believe kids want to learn about. The unfortunate result of that is that there are a hundred stories about Benjamin Franklin putting a key on a kite to "discover" electricity, but very few about the same individual starting the Philadelphia volunteer fire department, to say nothing of the poor, neglected glass armonica.

This is not to say your Ben Franklin kite story doesn't deserve to be heard—it does. However, as you research your topic, think of how you can make your kite story different from the rest of the books on that topic. What parts of the kite story are left out? What other experiments relate to that particular one? Are there other characters or experiences that you could add to make the story more relatable or provide a fresh perspective?

Choose a topic that excites children, but also take the time to discover why it excites them, and what you can do to keep that excitement going. But you don't have to be too quirky or cute or anything in particular to do so.

You Don't Have to be Avant-Garde (But You Can)

One complaint I frequently receive from individuals in the research stage is that they start to lose their motivation to write a book once they see how many other authors have already successfully covered the topic. I understand this—I have actually wailed piteously about the same thing.

The thing about writing anything at all—whether it's a picture book or your return address on an envelope—is that it will always be your own. Think of your favorite book. You will never write that book—it's already written. You will, however, write your own book. In your own words, from your own perspective, with a point of view that no book has ever considered before, your own book will radiate originality created by your own uniqueness.

As you mull over the topic for your children's book, I don't want you to seek discouragement. Don't compare your own talents to that of another writer. Compare your topic, your point of view, and the way in which you plan to tell your story, and allow their techniques to teach you and broaden your knowledge as a writer. But do not ever compare your writing to another writer. That other writer is already their own person, and while they might from time to time wish they had a clone, most of us really don't want to deal with the added responsibility.

Write your book, about your topic, from your perspective, for your audience. Most people have room for more than one book in their lives, after all. Can you even imagine a world in which we were only allowed to have one book on each topic?

All topics are new to children. As children's authors, I said earlier that I consider us "agents of discovery." No matter how much information young readers have about a certain topic—fiction or non-fiction—they are often quite hungry for more, like Carle's caterpillar. You have the chance to deliver tasty morsels that will help these very hungry readers and guide them toward finding more and more books that will encourage their growth.

Choosing a topic for an adult book isn't the easiest process in the world, but generally speaking, you have all the words and pages in the world to make your vision come to life. When selecting a topic for children, you have to put a little more thought into the process. There are certain words they won't understand—along with words they probably shouldn't hear. I'm no prude, but there's absolutely no logical reason to put crude language in a picture book intended for children (market it for adults, and I have no problem with it). You need to consider how you can introduce this brand-new mind to information in hopes that it will intrigue, fascinate, and entertain them.

It's not an easy task, which is why I recommend research. Before you fully commit to your topic, take it with you as you read lessons and books in your niche. Do the activities. Get on the same level as your audience so you can see what they see, and how they see it.

Then write your book so they can see even more.

Is It Age Group Appropriate?

When we use the phrase "age-appropriate," we tend to think of things like naughty language, adult scenarios, and violence. All of these things are very important considerations, but there's far more to writing an age-appropriate children's book than anatomical views and four-letter words.

Not so long ago, my little niece began showing interest in books. I would create a pile of picture books in front of her so she could choose whatever caught her fancy. She walked over to where I was sitting and grabbed the fondue recipe book I'd been skimming for dinner suggestions.

Originally, her mother and I thought it was because of the many bright pictures. The kid loves cheese, after all. So, I kept the fondue book with the children's book, and we pored over pages of melty cheese many times together.

But then she started bringing her own books. We figured she had grown out of her favorite book, but she also didn't show interest in any of the other kids' books I have—some of which were the same titles as her own books.

If you're a parent, you probably have this mystery solved, but it took Auntie a little while to catch on. It was the size and weight of the book. The fondue book was wide, thin, and flat with thick pages. Her own books were smaller paperbacks. Auntie has old hardback books from her childhood in the last century.

Age-group "appropriate-ness" absolutely includes language and themes, but when your reader is a small human with small hands and slowly developing coordination and strength, the size and shape of the book they're reading can also play a big part in how much they engage with the book. Why don't children read chapter books earlier? Because they can't lift them!

Of course, this also goes for the stuff inside the book. Choosing an age group for your book can be a triumphant moment because you're at last on track for your project. At the same time, it can feel quite restricting, because you'll have to play by a certain set of rules.

Let's take a look at some of the considerations when selecting an age group for your audience:

The Length of Your Book

Children truly have limited attention spans; additionally, they are very busy. With school, activities, friends, and family taking up a good portion of their day, it is important to note that not every child will have the ability to disappear for hours with a good book, regardless of how young you may have been when you discovered how joyful that particular activity could be.

As children grow, they gain the capacity for longer and longer spurts of reading, and they learn to appreciate a good bookmark so they can pause and restart their adventures whenever they have time.

The amount of time your audience will be willing to interact with your book grows as they do. Therefore, it's recommended that picture books be no longer than the amount of time it takes for a toddler to start wriggling in your lap. Novelty books should be long enough to allow a full adult discussion. Early and easy reading books can be challenging to finish in one reading session but should be simple to complete in two sessions. A good measurement for chapter books is one chapter a day, and we'll discuss what makes an appropriate-sized chapter next.

For the readers, this distinction is wonderful, because it ensures they are challenged without being completely overwhelmed. They have the opportunity to receive and digest information in a way that makes sense to them.

For writers, adhering to a particular length for your book can be really annoying. Many of us decide to write a children's book because we have wisdom and ideas we wish to pass on to future generations. However, I can tell you from experience that it is incredibly hard to put everything you want to say into just ten pages of print.

This is just one example of how topic and age group go hand-in-hand. You only have so much space to tell your tale, so it's important to choose a topic that will survive and thrive in the room available. But just as you can't actually build a functioning rocket in your backyard, you can't fully explain rocket propulsion in a handful of pages.

Don't forget—you're also supposed to be creative and have a unique perspective that is simultaneously entertaining and informative. Super easy, right?

Absolutely not. To be perfectly honest, I spend far more time planning a children's book than I do for a book intended for adult readers. If an adult book is an acre of prime farmland, a children's book is a container garden in the only corner of an apartment that has a window. It is entirely possible to make a story bloom and flourish like that container garden—you just have to be especially considerate in your planning and care for every last word just as you would care for every single seedling.

If your book is the garden, therefore, then your chapters are each stage of growth, making it our next stop on our list of age-appropriateness considerations.

Chapter Length

You may think this only applies to folks who write chapter books, but let's consider the function of a chapter. In books with a more complex plot, a chapter serves to drive the plot forward. Whether that includes developing a character, setting a location, or some type of action that drives the story onward, a chapter typically helps a reader become more involved in the story with further insight. The reader moves a step forward toward the realization or understanding they'll have at the end of the book when all adventures have been had and lessons learned.

Even though non-fiction books don't have a plot, information typically builds, and at the minimum, breaking that information into sections will go a long way toward helping readers find and understand the details they seek.

Think of chapters as scenes in movies. Some are a little longer than others, but whenever there is a break in action or a change in theme, the scene changes. Now think of the scenes in kids' movies versus the scenes in movies geared towards adults.

Musical cartoons always come to mind here, because the songs are often longer than the development of plot in between them. Consider that the classic Julie Andrews version of Mary Poppins is a 2-hour and 19-minute movie... with a 53-minute soundtrack recording. Plot happens quickly in media designed for children, and sometimes in the process of a song (or conversation, in traditional literature).

I like to think of picture books as having one chapter per page. My favorite example is the original Dick and Jane books. Between the illustrations and the words, each page is a pretty full journey. The conflict is pretty minor and the rising action is a little temperate by adult standards, but the idea is to teach children word recognition by presenting relatable scenarios. By making each page its own scene, younger children can learn to read by getting through as many pages as possible without losing track of a complicated plot.

Paragraph Size

Conventionally, we think of paragraphs as several sentences in length. I was taught that a paragraph is composed of 4-6 sentences that explore a single argument, idea or notion, depending on the length of the writing material.

However, this is not necessarily true for the younger set. Exploring a single concept per paragraph is the same, but the number of lines or words available for that exploration may be greatly restricted.

For the earliest children's books, a "paragraph" might be measured as a few letters or a single word. Ultimately, a paragraph serves as a transition from one idea development to another, so that could be as simple as "Look, Jane." and "Look, Dick."

Obviously, this does not meet the technical definition for a paragraph, and those of you who are deeply dedicated to grammatical rules might find yourself feeling offended here.

I am not suggesting that two words and two punctuation marks constitute a traditional paragraph. I am, however, encouraging writers who are gathering notes for their very first children's book to think of the overall impact of not only each word they write but how those words are grouped.

When children order a meal, we encourage them to take child-sized bites to prevent them from overwhelming their small esophagus and stomach—nobody wants choking or an upset stomach. Similarly, we can't throw an entire meatloaf of a book at a child and expect them to finish it in one sitting.

If we take a similar view towards writing for children, it makes a little more sense. An adult-sized bite/paragraph is larger than a child-sized paragraph because an adult can digest more words and concepts. Small children start with liquified and soft food because they lack the teeth to process it. Similarly, they should start with easy-to-digest literature.

At the same time, each of those small bite-sized tidbits of information has to explain everything that's going on to an audience who is very likely encountering some words in your book for the first time.

If that sounds horrible to you, fear not—practice and trying some of the exercises in this book will help this feel more natural. But first, let's break your text down even further...

Complexity of Sentences

Once upon a time in the early 1990s, my eighth-grade teacher taught me how to create compound-complex sentences with loads of clauses, and I never looked back.

While I actually won an award for my ability to string together an impressive tower of clauses back then, children will not give you praise for throwing a bouquet of semicolons at them. As a writer, you have to break down not just the information you feed your readers, but make sure the spoon you use to deliver their morsels isn't too big for their faces.

This was honestly a hard lesson for me to learn. I absolutely abhor short, choppy sentences. I feel like a sentence without proper descriptors feels naked and cold. Sometimes that's exactly the literary mechanism you want to use to drive home a point, but after a bit, the staccato repetitiveness of Dick and Jane starts to feel demanding and accusatory.

That, however, is my adult interpretation of the situation. I have several decades of practice under my belt. I don't struggle putting together that "l-o-o-k" is that thing I do with my eyes when I notice something new. I've already learned that stuff, so it's much easier for me to look at the symbols on the page and immediately understand what they mean.

The way you and I read and the way a child reads is different, plain and simple. While my brain sees short sentences and puts a tone on them, that's simply my brain. For a child, a two-word sentence may be a welcome reprieve from a challenging book.

Over the years, I've heard many first-time children's authors grouse about the limitations of short sentences and tiny paragraphs. "I would have understood my book when I was a ten-year-old. I don't know why all the beta readers are saying it's too long and complicated for a kid," they'll say.

I sympathize, of course. I was an insatiable reader. However, frequent readers are not the only kids buying books. Every child deserves the gift of literacy, and with that gift comes a nearly endless supply of information, adventures, and new experiences. If you're going to write a book for a certain audience, that's fantastic—just understand that the children who are not a part of that certain audience may not appreciate it on the same level.

A Child's Frame of Reference

Lastly, but certainly not least of your considerations when building a book for children, is the actual framework itself.

A child has an entirely different frame of reference for events than adults do. They work hard to grasp the people, objects, and events that occur in their world, but in those early years, that world is very, very small.

I once made a joke about Brussels sprouts to my assorted nieces and nephews ("What's the difference between Brussels sprouts and boogers? Kids never eat Brussels sprouts."). The older kids rolled their eyes with sad familiarity. The kids in the six-to-eight-year-old group hadn't necessarily tried Brussels sprouts, but they were aware that they were cabbage-y vegetables that a lot of folks don't like. The three-year-old looked at me very seriously and announced, "I don't know what that is, Silly! Tell a better joke." She then spun in her jelly shoes and flounced off with her Elsa dress billowing behind her.

To bring this back to the book you're writing: you have your topic, you've selected an appropriate age group for your topic, and now you have to pay attention not only to the way in which you arrange works onto the page but also the manner in which those words are arranged and how they're presented.

Little Steps for Little Books

By this point, I imagine we're all in agreement that writing a book for children has many more complicating considerations than most adult books. If you are feeling overwhelmed at this point (or at any point in the remainder of this book), please feel free to take a long deep breath and remind yourself that this only sounds unfamiliar because you haven't done it yet. Let's break it down into smaller pieces and put it all back together again.

First, we have the main concept of your book. Many people think of topics and content in terms of concepts children do and do not understand. I prefer instead to think of the depth to which they understand them.

For example, a very young child can recognize that this person is "Mommy" or that person is "Daddy." They don't necessarily have a concept of how these individuals relate to them or what they mean in their world, but they do know that Mommy and/or Daddy provide food, baths, clean diapers, and lots of love.

A slightly older child will be able to notice variations in this family structure. They might recognize that one of their playmates has only a Mommy or understand that another friend's Mommy didn't give birth to them, but she adopted them.

An even older child can understand that Mommy and Daddy are no longer married because they don't get along, or that their Mommy and Daddy adopted them because the people who gave birth to them couldn't take care of a baby.

The picture of life becomes more and more detailed as a child's experience in the world builds their frame of reference. A child needs to understand what it means to "get along" before they understand not getting along, for example.

As a writer, you can choose how much exposure and guidance you want to provide. There are some obvious choices here—a picture book focusing on spelling animal names should probably steer away from the topic of disease, for example. But let's say you're writing a Young Adult book for girls. Do you include natural but controversial topics like menstruation? Most teenagers are aware of bodily processes but also feel a certain amount of shame and embarrassment about them.

Ultimately, your ability to build your book within a child's frame of reference depends on your commitment to being their guide through this potential learning experience. Consider these examples, in which delicate topics are dealt with through different lenses:

1. Kimberly was late to Physics again, so Mr. Thompson was

already glaring at her before she even sat down. It wasn't her fault that Aunt Flo had decided to show up a few days early. It also wasn't Kimberly's fault that the building designer hadn't put a bathroom in the Science wing of the high school building.

2. Eddie didn't know what to do. Every time he thought of his Pop-Pop, he wanted to cry. He would never see Pop-Pop again. This made him want to see Pop-Pop even more. But Pop-Pop wasn't here anymore.

3. Jim did not like Harry. Harry was mean. Harry pushed Jim by the swings. Jim fell. All the children laughed. Jim hurt his knee when he fell. Jim told Mrs. Dickinson. "Harry pushed me," he said. "Harry is a bully."

What are your thoughts about each example? Who do you think each snippet was written for? What information do readers need to understand in order to empathize with the information provided? Can you think of a situation in which it would not be appropriate for a reader to come upon a passage like any of these?

Finding the Right Perspective : Simplify

The key to building upon a child's frame of reference is to explain things in a way that your audience can relate to. Children quite literally have a different perspective than adults do—generally a difference of a few feet. Staring out of a kitchen window has no meaning to a child who can't reach the kitchen counter. They're years from knowing what the view looks like because they need to grow tall enough to see it.

Writing for children is all about the art of introducing children to the world in a way they are prepared to receive it. With that comes appreciating the limitations to younger minds.

Perhaps the tree you would describe as "lustily verdant" in an adult book becomes "dark green like an emerald" to a younger audience, or simply "green" to an even younger group. Green starts out as just "green" for all of us. It's age, experience, and knowledge that allow us to see, understand, and use all of the many different shades for ourselves.

So how do we reframe our perspective to that of a child? We crouch down, and we approach the countertop from the viewpoint of the child who can't quite reach it. Literally and metaphorically.

As I mentioned earlier, research will help. Whether you have your own juvenile volunteers/consultants (mine have started charging an ice cream cone each time I need answers or information) or work strictly from the materials you find in your research, actually interacting with materials designed for your audience will help you understand the standard measurements for that frame, so to speak.

But as far as skills you can put in your toolbox for future projects, the objective here is to simplify:

1. Write

2. Read

3. Simplify

4. Read

5. Repeat until you run out of opportunities

When you look at the artwork in books intended for very young children, you'll notice the use of large, obvious shapes, familiar objects, and a limited palette of bright colors. According to the American Optometric Association, a child's vision is growing and changing along with them for the first two years of their life. Things like depth perception, color sensitivity, and the ability to coordinate eye and hand motion take time to fully develop.

As my niece proved with her fondness for my fondue book, bright, basic colors—like shiny fondue pots and serving ware—and a "just right" size-to-weight ratio for little hands are often more important than vocabulary choice or topic treatment.

Reframing for a child's perspective means not only simplifying the words we use and being cognizant of age-appropriateness. Instead, it means approaching your book from a simpler perspective.

As readers grow, so does their ability to see—physically and metaphorically. They start noticing details in artwork and nuances in words. They're ready to hear about what kind of green the tree is, and the objects you use to describe the green become more and more complex. Dark green, "green like an olive", "as green as the foam that floats on the sea", and "greener than a jealous crocodile" are all valid descriptions, but they appeal to different perspectives.

Simplifying your book to fit a child's frame of reference is perhaps the most complicated instruction I can give, and yet this skill is the center of being able to work very specifically within a very small space in a way that challenges the reader just enough to grow and develop into a wonderful human being.

Before you chuck this book in frustration, try practicing the art of simplification. The rules of this exercise are exactly as outlined above:

1. **Write-** exactly what you want the reader to know, no filter, no fuss. Just jot it down as it flows out of your brain.

2. **Read-** each and every word your brain supplied.

3. **Simplify-** by removing superfluous details and concepts that don't move the book along. If you're thinking "easy for you to say," then you have grasped the exact purpose of this exercise.

4. **Read-** the new version of your idea. Does it move the plot along? Does it help develop characters? Does it provide new information to the reader or help them gain a deeper understanding of information presented recently? Is it simply too darn long?

5. **Repeat-** the third step until you run out of opportunities.

In math class, we learned about reducing fractions. This is a similar exercise. You're essentially reducing your concept down to its central element.

But this isn't the end of things. From here, staring at the information you wish to convey, you can choose from a variety of building material to make that basic structure so much more interesting.

Insight into Kids and Books : The Experience of Space

When you open a book, any book, you'll notice that each page is composed of blank space, words, and potentially pictures or diagrams of some sort. Some of us get extra giddy when we see a page that's mostly words. Others prefer a greater amount of blank space. Others still are looking for the greatest number of illustrations.

I remember an early grade-school teacher chiding youngsters who preferred books with more blank space or pictures than words. But as I grow older, I wonder if perhaps she wasn't being a bit too harsh.

We all learn in different ways. Some of us prefer detailed text instructions. Some require elaborate visual instructions, while others prefer hands-on demonstrations.

Similarly, we process text differently. Blank space means "pause" in our minds. The spaces between words, sentences, and paragraphs help us understand where each thought begins and ends. Punctuation helps, of course, but many of us look to the white space as a place to rest and process whatever has come before it.

Some readers look forward to more blank space because that gives them more time to really work through what they've read. They might wish to read it aloud to themselves, draw a picture, or talk it out. More white space gives them more opportunities to hit that metaphorical pause button.

Readers who look for more words tend to be annoyed by pauses. They want their books in Big Gulp format, and they can put together more complex text all at once. The thing to look out for in this reading group is skimming and making assumptions. Granted, these skills helped me get through the semester of college when I signed up for three separate Shakespeare-oriented classes, but in the case of young readers, I have different feelings. Just as you wouldn't encourage children to chew their food quickly for the risk of choking, it's important for text-loving readers to slow down to properly digest their food. As a writer, that may mean chopping your content up to avoid rushing.

Those readers who are drawn to pictures aren't necessarily lazy, as my teacher assumed. It's far more likely that they're looking for visual cues that can help them process the subject matter. Sure, there comes a time when a reader should know enough of the words on the page to help them establish a mental image or understanding of what is happening in the book, but at the same time, we're always experiencing things for the first time.

How many times have you said something along the lines of, "I wish I had a picture because you'll never understand what it was like"? Perhaps your cat was making a funny face, or you managed to get your sleeve tangled on a doorknob in a particularly perplexing way—sometimes the things that happen in real life just have to be seen to be believed. This is exactly the role pictures play in books.

A picture of a red balloon labeled "red balloon" may seem like a sparse description, but there was a time when that was a lot of information, and putting the image with the words made all the difference. There is a time in everyone's life when all information is new, intriguing, and a little overwhelming.

Each page of your book is an opportunity to connect with your audience, regardless of what age group you write for. Varying up the blank space and massive blocks of text is important for all readers; however, younger readers have significantly less capacity for marathons of relentless runes.

Similarly, the actual font, text size, and page/font color can have a huge impact on your reader. Educators and medical experts have argued for years about whether single or double spacing is better for the eyes and the mind. With greater research and attention being placed on neurodivergent conditions, we're also learning that how text looks can actually impact how it is processed and understood by different individuals.

Larger fonts have long been the go-to for younger readers. Not only are large, bold letters easier to read visually, but they are easier to interact with. Consider the difference between these two examples:

fox

FOX

One is abundantly clearer than the other. One is highly stylized, while the other uses box letters that cannot be mistaken for other letters. Furthermore, one is just the right size for tracing fingers over the letters while trying to sound them out.

You are likely a very long way from worrying about the layout of your book, but I wanted to mention the significance of white space in the same breath as discussing book, page, paragraph, and sentence length.

For many of us, a book is more than just words on a page—it's a full life experience. As you build your children's book, keep in mind that you're building more than a story. This is an interactive journey, and as the author, you're the leader, builder, teacher, and entertainer. Therefore, it's your responsibility to take each of those roles seriously.

Chapter Two

Choosing the Right Words to Write Children's Books

When we're building a book for children, we must select the correct building materials. Books are built from words, but children's books in particular are often made of a combination of words and pictures. While the main focus of this chapter will be on the words, this chapter's *Insight* section is all about pictures. This is not to minimize the role pictures play in children's books, but because I am a writer and this is a "how to write" book, I'll let the "how to illustrate" folks share their own expertise!

Words are hugely important to every book, of course. Writers are creators, and words are our medium. Folks who do a lot of writing tend to know a lot of words. They can put them together in interesting ways to create a detailed picture of a situation, but they can also use them in many other ways.

Here are three sentences that more or less say the same thing:

- The words I choose and the order in which I encourage you to read them have a significant impact on your interpretation and understanding of the topic.

- When I put words on the page, I do so in a way that maximizes the experience for you, as far as putting meaning to those words and allowing you to personally process them through your own lens, but I also provide my bias to ensure you appreciate them contextually to the rest of the book.

- Writers manipulate their readers through word choice.

As you can see, the words you use matter a lot, even when writing for fellow adults. In the first sentence, I am your charming host and guide through this book. In the second sentence, I'm purposefully trying to confuse the reader while making them feel comforted. In the third sentence, I specifically chose words that might make you feel a little uncomfortable about the overall relationship between reader and writer.

At the end of the day, though, we as writers have to appreciate that we are in control of the book. We paint the pictures, we arrange the building blocks, and readers will get the story we place on the page for them. Folks who are involved in editing, publishing, or marketing your book may disagree to a certain extent, but ultimately, your book is your story in your words, written by you.

Therefore, when writing specifically for young readers, we need to be just as conscious of our words and their meaning as we would be in a book for adults, if not more so. The things we read as children often get stuck in our heads forever.

Have you ever wondered why red balloons frequently show up in children's literature? Balloons come in infinite colors, patterns, and designs, and yet when you take a deeper glance at the appearance of balloons in children's books, television, and movies, the balloon often shows up as a big round rubbery version—and more often than not, in a crimson hue.

If you do a little peeking into symbolism, a red balloon signifies childhood innocence, hope, and a carefree attitude. As a writer, I can't help but wonder which came first in this chicken/egg scenario—is the red balloon used frequently in media because of its symbolism, or did its symbolism develop because of how frequently a red balloon appears in media?

Point being—the words, images, and scenarios that are presented to us as children stay with us through adulthood. Anyone who has read the book *IT* by Stephen King or watched any of the film iterations will surely tell you that something even as basic as a red balloon can have a deep psychological impact on young readers well into adulthood. (For those who have not read *IT* the book, a red balloon is one of the indicators that the chief antagonist is lurking about, and is in no way malicious itself, but a tool King uses to build suspense. No spoilers!)

The words you write become reality for the reader. When your reader is very young, their reality is very small—though certainly not for lack of trying to push boundaries.

Let's take a look at some of the things to keep in mind when you're choosing those words to build that reality.

Vocabulary Building Blocks

For most writers, the fact that you can't use a full-blown adult vo-cabulary in a children's book is more or less intuitive. After all, most writers were children, if they aren't still in some way, shape, or form. Furthermore, we are all still learning and growing as human beings throughout our lives, and it stands to reason that nearly every day you and I will encounter at least one word we've never heard before.

One thing that children's authors ought to consider is how we learn language. We're certainly not born speaking eloquently, and it's years before our little fingers are capable of holding a writing utensil, much less wiggling it on paper to make discernable symbols. Understanding how words are gathered by children can help us not only write what they know, but help them grow.

Definition, Description, Context, and More : How to Build with Words

As children, we learn new words in many ways. At school, we're given spelling and vocabulary lists, which were hands down my favorite lessons. My editors likely won't believe this, since they only see my typos, but I was a fiend for spelling and vocab as a child. While I was always picked last for team sports, I was heavily recruited when it came to spelling and vocabulary games. Many writers, editors, and word-smiths of all types find themselves in this category as well. Learning the definitions of new words opened our worlds.

Taking a word apart to memorize it letter by letter, phonetic sound by the syllable, definition, and usage was a magical process to my younger self. I think I understand how master chefs feel as they prepare a new dish, ingredient by ingredient, savoring each step of the experience.

However, it has come to my attention that not everyone's spelling and vocabulary lists are the highlight of their week. For every child who loves their vocab, there are just as many children who mentally delete their list as soon as the test is over. We all only have so much capacity for learning and retaining, and as I've said before, children are absolutely inundated with new information. It is quite understandable if some of it doesn't stick right away.

Therefore, as writers, we have the opportunity to reinforce knowledge and help children ease this new information into their worlds.

I know I just said that the words we write become reality, but it's not so much the words themselves. It's the meaning of the words as a group, as a whole, that create that reality. It's not the words "r-e-d b-a-l-l-o-o-n" but the image we have of that big, round, crimson thing floating around on the end of a string. Use the word b-l-u-e, and the whole scene changes. The words provide the information that creates this reality.

We call that information a "description." Most of us use description without thinking too much about it. Just now, in my description of balloon, you were able to contextualize both a red and blue balloon based on a single simple adjective.

Your words can paint even brighter pictures for children, too, just by using description. Let's say you're trying to help a child understand a fire truck. For early readers, you can get away with saying it's a "big red truck that firefighters drive." But at some point, your reader can have their horizon expanded to understand that there are also ladders, pressure valves, hose connections, and a variety of tools on a fire truck. You can tell them facts, such as "this valve does this, and this connection is used to do another thing." Or, you can describe them.

"Dave the fire fighter connects the hose here. He needs to monitor this dial to make sure..." etc.

Consider how you can use description in your book to explore situations. There are so very many adult terms that we just don't realize children may not be able to understand right away.

Take this list of words as an example. I've received feedback in the past about using these words in material intended for children, and I think they're right. There might even be a few you don't recognize as an adult:

- Shut-off valve

- High beams

- Belay

- Garbage disposal

- Test tube

- Owl pellet

- Tire rotation

- Saddle

As you ponder this list, consider how you might use description to explain these terms to children. None of them are particularly difficult, but if you've never had exposure to any of these things, you might not know exactly what's involved. But as writers, we get the real treat of explaining it to young readers in a way that will immediately catch them up. Description can be an easy way to give them the details.

Another common way children learn new words is through context. Perhaps the easiest way to show how learning through context works would be to refer you to an episode of the classic television show, *Sesame Street*. Letters and words are shown in writing, in colors, in song, in person (a walking, talking puppet who is a letter of the alphabet? Why not!), in skits, and so forth.

If you plan to write for children, you will need to surrender to context in some regard. Whether that means planning pictures or losing a few words or paragraphs to explaining a particular concept, you'll want to slow down to make sure everyone is following along.

There are several ways to do this. Much of the time, you can seamlessly give a word or concept contextual definition without actually pointing it out.

For example, let's say, "Hazy the cat had a terrible stench." The possibly troublesome word here is "stench." As adults, we know that Hazy is a stinky cat, but depending on where a young reader is on their learning journey, they may not be aware.

At the same time, "stench" is a fantastic word to learn, especially for kids who enjoy coming up with good insults.

So what if we say instead: "Hazy the cat had a terrible stench. He smelled worse than old garbage and the sewer combined. People covered their noses as they passed his favorite spot on the fence."

The context there lets the reader know that "stench" has something to do with a really bad smell. It's not obvious, nor intrusive—it's a continuation of Hazy's description.

Additionally, this context is correct and direct. If a child were to look up the word "stench" in a dictionary or dictionary app, they would learn that stench means "a strong and unpleasant smell." (That definition, in particular, came from the Cambridge dictionary online, if you're curious.)

Essentially, as a writer you must balance what children are likely to understand with things that might be unfamiliar. In the case of Hazy the cat, I took a bet that children would be aware of what old garbage and the sewer smelled like, even if they weren't familiar with the word "stench." No matter what kind of life you've had so far, you've likely encountered stinky trash or backed up plumbing. The combination of description and context helps the reader connect immediately with the word "stench," for better or worse for the playground insult scene.

When you're setting up context to introduce something that might be new to a young reader's world, it's important to start with something they do know. The tricky part is figuring out what they do know. In Hazy's case, that's not too difficult—anyone who has spent time on a playground will tell you that kids have a pretty good running memory of things that are gross. But what about a concept that's more specialized.

Here's a mini-exercise for you to help illustrate this point: Let's say you're writing a children's book about a specific animal. How would you explain things like tentacles, beaks, talons, and hooves to someone who has no idea what those things look or feel like?

Take a moment, if you like, to jot down some ideas. How would you explain the texture of different animals, or the way they move? Context can help. Comparisons to more familiar things can help. Pictures can also help, or tactile examples—*Pat the Bunny*, anyone?-- can be even more helpful.

Let's give this a quick try to get you started in practicing the art of describing things for new readers. For the purpose of this mini-exercise, let's describe a dish sponge. As you practice, you can absolutely choose whatever object you like—I generally start with things on my desk. But for the purpose of uniting us all with a common object, we'll start by listing off all the properties of the object you use to clean all the crusty stuff from your dishes.

My dish sponge is:

- Stinky

- Faded green

- Supposed to look like a sloth

- Hanging from a peg in my sink

- Has a soft side and a rough scrubby side

- Overdue for replacement

Children know what stinky is, and the green part is pretty straight-forward. But "faded?" "Sloth?" "Scrubby side?" "Replacement?" These are the kind of things that very young readers might not understand.

But what if I wrote instead: "My dish sponge is light green. It's stinky because I use it every single day. One side of the sponge is soft like a towel. The other side is rough and scratchy. I use that side to help scrape off food that gets stuck to my dishes."

Practicing descriptions like this will help you become more aware of whether your words are connecting with your readers—and audiences will certainly let you know when you've missed the connection. Young readers are not afraid of providing honest opinions about books, including a list of words or ideas they didn't understand.

So what should you do? Avoid multi-syllabic words at all costs? Include illustrations with absolutely everything you write? Decide to abandon your plans to write a children's book and stare into the abyss until you no longer feel the urge to write a children's book?

While all of these are possibilities, you do have options that are simpler and less agonizing.

Glossaries and Reference Sections

Adding a glossary to a book for youngsters can be a win-win situation for the writer and the reader. By adding a list of key terms and their definitions, you make no assumptions about what your reader is and is not familiar with. It is their choice to flip to the end of the book to check out the glossary, but if memory serves, this is a rather popular option for text books throughout the schooling process.

But then there's the matter of what to put in the glossary. In theory, you can put any word you wish in the glossary. At the same time, you also need to acknowledge the book/glossary ratio. If you're explaining the book more than you're developing the book itself, perhaps there is an opportunity to reevaluate some of the word choices you've made.

At the same time, there are situations in which a thorough glossary is a must. Non-fiction books in particular benefit from a list of terms and definitions, especially those in areas like science, history, sports, or arts, in which there might be quite a bit of niche terminology that needs to be explained.

There are opportunities for glossaries in fiction books, as well. As they grow, children are beginning to take interest in hobbies. They might be fascinated by sailing, or football, or basket weaving, or horticulture, or quite literally anything going on in the world around them that captures their fancy. As a result, kids tend to devour books about their favorite topics with particular fervor.

This trend can start in the picture book stages, but usually manifests in full around the beginner chapter book stage of reading development. Children who have an affinity for a specific topic will gravitate towards books that are related in any way to their passion. And rightly so—we want them to gain that knowledge and develop the unquenchable thirst for more.

However, it can be difficult to write a book about a niche topic without excluding readers who are at different stages of their quest for information. That is to say, no matter what you write, there will be readers who have been doing that for years, and there will be some who have no way of visualizing what you're writing about.

An example I like to use here is that of driving a car with a manual transmission. I choose this example specifically because of a real-life situation in which my cousin and I attempted to move my auntie's car in her driveway. Our auntie simply handed us the key with the request to move the car into the garage. Having two legal driver's licenses between us, my cousin and I set off to do just that.

Except we couldn't get the engine to turn over. We turned the key, jammed on the gas, turned it on and off. It didn't seem to be the battery, because the lights and radio came on. After about 20 minutes of frantic pondering and attempted problem-solving, my cousin and I returned to the house defeated.

That was when we both learned that in cars with a manual transmission, you have to press on the clutch as you start the ignition. The omission of that critical piece of information is what turned a simple request into a story that is still told at family gatherings to this day.

What I'm saying is that when writing a book that fits into a niche topic, it is better to assume that it is your reader's first-time learning about that topic rather than to force them to rely on external sources in order to understand your book. Remember what we discussed regarding attention spans? A quick peek to an online dictionary is fine, but it's far better to have key terms defined by description, definition, context, picture, or glossary than to force your reader to keep running to reference sources in order to understand your book.

My personal favorite choice for optional reader edification is the References section. We call these "Works Cited" and "Bibliographies" and "Sources" sections as adults, but the "Where to Learn More" section just sounds more exciting, especially for a young mind on a quest for more details.

Yes, tracking down references does require extra effort on behalf of the reader. They'll either have to click or copy a link, or find a particular book. It's definitely not for the faint of heart, and as you're compiling a reference section for children, you may wonder many times why you're doing this in the first place.

Most likely, it's because if you weren't the child who loved the References section, you knew the kid who did. All around the world, there is a certain group of children and adults alike who love the opportunity to learn more about a topic that currently has their fascination.

Furthermore, you can use these external sources to illustrate a point that words and illustrations cannot. For example, you can link to a video that shows how fast a horse can run, or an article that includes a diagram of the different types of roses, or a recipe for pumpkin pie for those who have never tasted it.

If you choose to add a section that leads to additional reference material, you'll need to consider how to organize it. The rules aren't the same for a children's book as they are for a scientific study, so you don't necessarily need to create footnotes for a picture book. However, if you know a few extra materials that are designed specifically for children to interact more with your topic, it is a nice bonus. Parents will thank you for giving them extra material to feed their child's obsession — and their own.

The title of this section refers to vocabulary building blocks, and I might have slightly manipulated your perception by talking about spelling and vocabulary lists first. For children, vocabulary extends far beyond knowing the difference between "lightning" and "lightening." It means more than turning "yummy" into "delicious" into "delectable" into "ambrosial." It is giving words to the things that exist in that child's world that they do not know how to describe. You are giving them these words for the first time—you are defining a new experience with your words.

Perhaps that sounds more serious than it is. After all, the likelihood of a child remembering every single book they read during their formative years is pretty slim. But while your book may not be the title they remember forever, it will be through the pages of your book that they continue their journey to learn more about their favorite topic and the world around them.

Now I'd like to continue with a little more conversation around the topic of detail and description. While description can be used to define new words and terms, it can also be used to share with the reader how things look, sound, smell, taste, and feel. It is descriptions that awaken the senses through simple letters on a page, and one of the most important ways writers connect with readers.

Painting the Right Level of Detail

Earlier we discussed being able to write things in a manner that children can relate to—the process of simplifying our concepts, plot, and even descriptions so that younger readers can understand what we're trying to convey.

But to say that adding description to a children's book is just a matter of putting the right modifier in the right place is to thoroughly downplay the act that you are about to undertake.

Writing a children's book is an acrobatic task that involves equal parts art and science. Whoever said, "Brevity is the soul of wit," has never had a child follow up their explanation with "why?" or "how?" or "what does that mean?"

There is a certain stage in every child's life in which no fact can be taken for granted. The sky cannot simply be blue; instead, children in this stage will need to discuss water droplets, convection, and those light spectrum wavelengths we talked about earlier. But the caveat here is that of all of that, water droplets will be the easiest concept for a child in this stage to understand.

Where to Start with Modifiers

As a children's author, you need to be able to describe a scene, a character, an object, a building, the way a train sounds, quite honestly everything in a manner that is:

- Not too short, because they'll skim over it

- Not too long because they'll ignore it

- Uses words they already know

- Describes concepts they are already familiar with or

- Provides enough context to be understood

- But seriously isn't too long—you also have an overall word count to think about here

At a certain stage in life, children have a lot of elementary concepts about a great many things. They know a solid amount about their immediate surroundings, a few things about the world outside of that, and a scattering of trivia about the world outside of that. They are also trapped by two equal and opposing forces: The desire to learn more about this topic and the inexplicable need to keep moving.

The child who chooses to read your book is the one who caved to the desire to learn more. However, you aren't out of the woods yet, so to speak! You only have each reader's attention on a word-to-word basis, and if you go on for three paragraphs about how fluffy the kitty is, you may find a lot of bookmarks permanently resting there.

When writing a book for young readers, I would consider the urgency of your modifiers. Is it more important for your reader to understand:

- "Tim ran towards the gymnasium door. He was not very fast."

- "Tim ran slowly and awkwardly towards the gymnasium door."

or

- "Tim was not athletically inclined. In fact, he ran a lot like the gears of a clock. All of his pieces went in different directions at different times. His left arm did a clockwise whirling motion while his right one did a flapping thing with his hand fully outstretched at shoulder height. His legs seemed to argue about which direction they were heading. As a result, it took Tim a few moments to get to the gymnasium door."

Either of these descriptions are technically appropriate for a children's book. The vocabulary isn't too challenging, and each option provides adequate information about what is happening.

That being said, consider how you would use each description in a book. Which one do you feel would be most appropriate for your intended audience? What makes the other two options less ideal for a book in your selected reading group?

There are, of course, no "right" or "wrong" answers to these questions, but these are the types of things I recommend considering as you work on your text. Sometimes brevity is the actual soul of wit, and a shorter description would perfectly underscore how incredibly uncoordinated Tim is. Similarly, using the longer description might work very well in a picture book, where children could see poor Tim trying to keep his balance as his body betrays him. What makes the difference—and what should ultimately be your deciding factor in what type of description you choose—is your audience.

Ask the Experts

I have found over the years that the best way to describe things to children is to understand how children describe things.

Our adult minds know too much, and they process things with far too much clarity sometimes. As a result, we find ourselves completely taken aback by the way children process the same things.

I was happily celebrating a family Easter dinner with a shameless number of deviled eggs when my niece, age 5, approached me. "Why do you have so many cut off lady heads around here?" she asked, completely benignly.

Understandably, every member of my family became concerned to a very high degree. The explanation, however, had to wait, because I couldn't stop giggling.

You see, my great-grandmother was a beautician. She owned a beauty parlor, and in addition to doing the hair growing out of peoples' heads, she made wigs. As a result, she owned several gorgeous wig form heads. When she passed, I kept them as a memento.

My mistake was that I put them in my office, and during the family celebration, I let the kids into my office to play on the computer, watch TV, and play with my art supplies. It didn't occur to me that not everyone would understand wig forms, or why I would have a bunch of bald women's faces/heads in my office.

None of the adults had thought anything of them, because we all had some concept of what they were. For some reason, we see a ton of them at Midwestern flea markets and antique malls. It wasn't until a child had explained it in a way she could understand- "cut off lady heads"- that we all realized that they probably would appear strange to someone who had no perspective on the matter.

The same is true of how you color your children's book. You only have so much space and only so many words to really give your reader the experience you want them to have. Therefore, you need to discover which combination of words has the greatest impact on the reader. The best option here is to go right to the source.

Now I'm sure there are several of you who might be thinking, "I don't understand. I spent my entire childhood in Booth 9A at Apple Valley Peddler's Swap. My entire existence has been based on Old People's Old Stuff. Why wouldn't kids today know about a flea market?"

To be perfectly honest, I understand and appreciate this point of view. Some of my happiest childhood memories involve antiquing with my grandparents. This is a perfect example of why it's important to go directly to the source.

By "the source," I mean connecting with actual children. I've mentioned this several times now, but I'd like to dig a little deeper into the concept when considering vocabulary and word choice.

Becoming a Child to Write for a Child

Presumably, your readers will speak the language in which your book is written. That means you'll all have access to the same dictionary, the same basic words, letters, and so forth.

However, just as crossing the county or state line might mean a shift in accent, language use also changes between generations. For example, at the time I am writing this book, "Ohio" is currently an adjective used to describe a barren wasteland, despite having been exclusively a noun since it became a territory following the American Revolutionary War- at least, as far as I'm aware. In fact, it's become a nuisance word that teachers and educational administrators have banned from use.

If this fate can befall the 17th State of the United States of America, imagine what could happen to the many English words that actually do have multiple interpretations?

In the last section, we talked about research from the perspective of gathering material for your topic. Ok, perhaps we've talked about research a lot, but this is the final time I'll mention it in any type of detail.

Research can help you figure out what words to use when discussing the topic of your choice. Whether you actually meet up with children and interact with them, read books and magazines geared towards children, watch kids' movies and television shows all day, or download lesson plans to help you appreciate the vocabulary level of your intended readers, I'd like to take a moment to highlight the many reasons why doing as many of these as possible is so important.

In no particular order:

    1. **Vernacular**- Vocabulary lists will only highlight existing

words in the context in which they were intended. In the 1980s and 1990s, upper level words like "bodacious" and "egregious" were made popular by movies like *Bill & Ted's Excellent Adventure* and popular children's characters like the Teenage Mutant Ninja Turtles.

Years ago, we had to do a ton of research to figure out if that was really what the kids were calling it these days. Today, we just need to tune in to children's broadcasting on PBS, Disney, or Nick in order to watch children of all age groups interacting. Or even better—simply type in a very direct search criteria, like "video of a six-year-old's birthday party" and have dozens of videos delivered via YouTube.

2. Interaction- Kids talk to each other differently than they speak with adults. Furthermore, they interact with familiar kids and adults in a far different way than they do with strangers. Some are shy, some are eager to share, and in the case of my nephew, some decline to participate by running away.

As you're preparing to write your children's story, think about the scenes where children speak to each other or adults. What is the relationship between these individuals? Where can you watch a similar interaction? Being able to recreate these interactions warmly and accurately through your writing will help children connect more personally with your book.

3. How things exist in a child's world- How would you describe holding a baby chicken in your hand? Off the top of my head, I might say a baby chick is yellow and fuzzy, with sharp tiny feet and a beak. My six-year-old niece, on the other hand, will inform you that chickies are wobbly and mean. When she was holding one at the science museum, it darted around her hand, almost fell off, and pecked at her when she caught it from falling.

As writers, we meet our young audience where they are in their knowledge, then guide them to a greater understanding of the whys and hows. Baby chickens can be yellow and fuzzy as well as wobbly and mean. By giving context to why the chickie was wobbly and mean—"it's scared and wasn't sure if you were going to hurt it"-- my niece was then able to reform her understanding of what these tiny birds are. "They're just cute little babies trying to figure it out," she said afterwards. "And they're fluffy yellow cutie-wooties, super cute and fluffy." She then continued to make up a song about baby birds, which soon dissolved into a tune about her brother eating boogers.

Thus is the accurate reality of a child, and your job, as a children's author, is to determine how to capture and connect with that exact type of energy.

As you read this list—and dare I say, this entire section—you may have noticed a lot of parallels with the last section. This is correct. The process of writing a children's book is similar to the process of writing anything, in that you have to keep a lot of metaphorical plates spinning at different levels and speeds as necessary for the overall message of the book. The number of plates is dictated by the reading level of your audience, but any writer/professional plate spinner can tell you that a single spinning plate is more than enough.

Yes, we're talking about the same concepts, but I'm changing the way we address each concept slightly. When writing your first children's book, you'll have to think about all of these things consciously and simultaneously in order to remember them all. You might find yourself second-guessing every syllable.

With time and practice, however, it becomes easier to put all of this together. As adults, it's hard to put ourselves back into the mindspace of childhood. In fact, many of us have good reason to avoid revisiting our own childhood experiences. At the same time, it's important to tap into that type of naive innocence within ourselves in order to be able to become an "agent of discovery" for our young readers.

Yes, choosing the right words is important because you want your reader to understand them, but it's also important for your reader to be able to appreciate each scene or scenario in your book as well.

Watching the Words Go By

Then there's the matter of pacing. As if choosing the right words to say and describe things wasn't hard enough, you have to be certain to use your words in just the right way that your audience isn't left struggling to follow along.

When we're writing for other adults, many of us establish a pace similar to how we would naturally converse with each other. If we were to have a face-to-face conversation, I would speak to you very much as I'm writing for you now. There would probably be far more jokes and asides, but I would attempt to provide you with detailed explanations without explaining you into latter stages of acute boredom.

But when we have conversations with children, they're entirely different, aren't they?

To demonstrate, here's a transcript of a conversation I had with my nephew- age 5- about dinosaurs:

Me: Oh hey, Nephew! What's that toy?

Nephew: It's Ankylosaurus.

Me: Is that a dinosaur?

Nephew: Yes, but it's name is Ankylosaurus. Look! You can see because he has these spikes here on his back.

Me: Cool! What do those spikes do?

Nephew: Um, he also has this big tail. RAWR!!

Me: That is a big tail. What else about Ankylosaurus?

Nephew: I... have. RAWR! It's Ankylosaurus. And, um. He's got this (points to tail) and this (points to spikes).

Me: Is he your favorite?

Nephew: He's from the Chewtashious Zone. (note: this was later translated by his mother as "Cretaceous Period")

Me: Where's that?

Nephew: RAWR! (mimics dinosaur attack with the toy)

So what are some observations we can make about a conversation with a 5-year-old about a topic they are passionate about?

Personally, I was impressed that he knew the name of Ankylosaurus—and he pronounced it correctly! Apparently there is a character he loves who is, in fact, an Ankylosaurus, and his devotion to the character led him to learn more about the dinosaur. This, in my opinion, is the goal of children's media—to encourage more learning and growth.

But there are other things worth noticing in this conversation. My nephew didn't actually want to talk about Ankylosaurus; he wanted to tell me things he knew about Ankylosaurus in order of importance to him. He was also overwhelmed by the urge to play with his toy several times instead of just standing there talking to a silly old adult about it.

When you're establishing the pace in a children's book, you can't always rely on the concept of having a conversation with the audience. You need to actively work to keep the discussion going while simultaneously curating and continuing interest in the topic at hand. I have never personally tried juggling while riding a unicycle, but I imagine the required levels of concentration, skill, and frustration are similar.

So, in that vein, let's take a look at pacing, and how to keep children alert and interested from page one to "The End."

The Difference between Too Fast and Too Slow

On Monday morning, Nancy woke up with bad breath. She knew she
had a math exam that day, but she was really looking forward to talking
to her friend Henrietta after school. They had a whole bunch of stuff
going on in their lives, like cheerleading and also the big school dance
coming up.

By Thursday afternoon, Nancy was exhausted and hadn't even had
the chance to talk to Henrietta. Now the big cheerleading competition
was just two days away!

Wait, what?

Have you ever found yourself reading a book, and suddenly the
time line shifts, leaving you with more questions than answers? What
happened Monday? Why didn't Nancy get to speak to Henrietta?
What did she need to talk to her about, anyway? Why is this the first
we're hearing about the cheerleading competition? What happened
to the math test? Is the bad breath significant?

Children's books cannot be infinite in length, for obvious reasons.
Therefore, we sometimes need to hit the fast-forward button to skim
over a span of time between two significant events. However, there are
times when going too quickly leaps over too many details that—while
not necessarily essential to moving the story forward—can help the
reader better relate to what is happening or what is about to happen.

But then we have the exact opposite:

It was exactly 6:31am when Nancy woke up on Monday morning.
She wasn't looking forward to the day, but she was excited about talking
to her friend Henrietta later. She had a math exam right before lunch,
which meant she probably wasn't going to take her full lunch break.
She always took her time on math tests, checking and double-checking
her answers. Math wasn't always her strongest subject, and she didn't
want to fall behind. She did that once in seventh grade, and it had
been disastrous. She had to take Algebra twice just to understand the

whole concept of equations. Now, as a new freshman at Clingman High, Nancy was looking forward to keeping her grades up as she considered her college options.

Nancy was really interested in a career in fashion design, and the schools she had in mind probably wouldn't be excited about a student with a C- average in math. Fashion design doesn't really require trigonometry, Nancy thought to herself. But my teeth are disgusting.

If you were silently screaming "ok, get on with it!" please know that I was, too. All of this information about Nancy is really great, and establishes a lot about who she is as a person, but we're not really getting anywhere here. If this is a book about teenagers coping with the stress of math tests and preparing for college, it might be important, but the reader is about to forget about Henrietta.

As children's authors, we only have so many pages, paragraphs, and words to capture our readers' attention and carry it through. It's easy to lose readers of any age, but children are especially prone to getting lost. The speed and rhythm of your writing will help keep them on the right trail, enjoying the scenery at a just-right learning speed.

When to Explain...

For many writers, slowing down is easier than speeding up. After all, a lot of us are admittedly verbose in our day-to-day existence.

Furthermore, many of us come with a built-in need to explain everything to its last molecule. In scenarios where you're quite literally speaking to someone who has no idea what you're talking about, it is a common phenomenon to give in to the desire to over-explain.

Consider, if you will, everything closest to your right hand at this exact moment. I currently have Jim the cat supervising me from a box next to my computer monitor. In the box is an old orange t-shirt.

There's my mouse and my mousepad, a very large plastic cup that holds my drinking water, and a painted tile coaster preventing the very large cup from leaving very large rings on my desktop. I've got a chewed up black pen, a small notebook with a drawing of a taco on the front, and a squeezy stress toy that looks like a rainbow-colored unicorn.

All of these things are real and relevant to my working environment, and each has actually had an impact on my writing, whether directly or indirectly. But which of these details do I need to share in order for my readers to understand this book?

What you choose to explain in detail in a children's book depends on this essential question: what is the most important thing for the reader to know at the end of the book?

As my reader, you don't need to know about Jim the cat or my desk. You just need to know my thoughts on writing a children's book, and how these thoughts might inspire you in your endeavors. The most important thing about my desk is the part that you see—the words on the page.

Think of each page of your children's book as a single scene, just like my desk, or whatever is going on near your right hand. It's important to the overall existence of the scene, but not every little detail needs to be accounted for. When writing a children's book, it's important to explain only what the reader needs to learn in order to understand the book.

So how do you know you've accomplished that? The only sure way is to get reader feedback, but it is possible to build yourself a grid in order to measure your pace.

This is a little more formulaic than I am typically, but oddly enough, this piece of advice has stood the test of time from my early Language Arts papers in the late 1980s to the book you are reading today. Which is to say, the person responsible for teaching me is likely enjoying a well-deserved retirement and is completely unconcerned with any feedback you might have about their methodology. If this grid system doesn't work for you—and it might not—focus instead on the overall concept and see what you can bring forth with your own particular skills and habits.

You don't have to call it a grid, either. A ladder, a lattice, a support structure, a measuring system... any of these terms could apply. I like to think of it as a grid-like structure, like scaffolding, that can be moved about to support the overall building process without actually changing the principles of design. I know that sounds a bit vague, so keep reading. Grab a notepad or note-taking device while you're at it, so you can play along.

The first step to creating this magical structure that will help guide the pace of your book is to know exactly what you want your reader to learn by the end of the book. This could be as simple as "D-O-G means dog; refers specifically to the creature pictured in the book." This could be as complicated as, well, literally anything and everything that happens in the hallways of a high school. Whatever the overall goal or lessons of your book may be—whether one or many—jot them down first. If your book is still very much in the hypothetical stages, but you want to try this yourself, feel free to invent a topic.

Now it's time to decide how to get there. What do we need to know in order to get from the dedication page of your book to the final page, when everything comes together?

Start with the big things—the largest events of your book. For example: In order to understand why President Abraham Lincoln was assassinated, you need to understand the meaning of the Civil War. In order to understand the Civil War, you need to understand why the North and the South disagreed with each other. In order to understand that disagreement, you need to have an idea of what slavery is, which in turn requires a little bit of comprehension on the matters of world geography, politics, and human rights. Make notes of all of these steps (even if they're still for an imaginary book).

Alright, now let's turn our attention to your book. How much space do you have for this book? You don't necessarily have to consider the size of each physical page, but how many pages or even words do you have available for your story? While page number is always at the discretion of the author, take the time to research how long other books in your genre and reading level are on average. If you're working on a make-believe book, choose the approximately length of the childhood book you imagine your book would be most like.

And now the mathematical part. It's not so much algebra as geometry, in my opinion, since you're looking at each bit of information you need to include in your book, and figuring out how much space you can give it. How much do you need to include about world geography versus the concept of slavery if you were writing the Abraham Lincoln example I provided? Would you review the plot of "Our American Cousin," or simply leave things at "he was at the theatre"?

... And When to Fast-Forward

So therefore, you will sometimes need to gloss over bits and chunks here and there.

By "gloss over," I don't mean you should just drop entire facts or refuse to explain things that might need at least a little extra context. Instead, don't spend time on things that aren't essential.

Unfortunately for most of us, everything seems very essential at first. As an author, we start with a very clear picture of the journey we want to take our reader upon, and the fact that it simply doesn't fit into a perfect 20 page book is largely unfair. I understand.

This is when I revisit the grid (or whatever you've chosen to call it). If I look at the structure I've built, based on the main concept of my book and the many additional details that make that concept understandable, I will often see that some of those details aren't quite as crucial as others. They don't require as many words to explain, or they can be easily expounded upon through context—remember our discussion about context?

Sometimes you don't need to fret upon a detail as much as you would like. I'll never forget the panic I felt when I was tasked with explaining the concept of a saddle to very small children. There are several different types of saddles, which do several different things depending on a variety of factors, right? But if you simplify it to its most recognizable state, a saddle is simply "what we put on a horse when we're going to ride it," especially in the context of a book about horses. The difference between a Western saddle and an English saddle might be significant in the world as a whole, but maybe not so much in a book introducing children to the very concept of a horse.

Creating a grid offers me an opportunity to visualize how much room I have for the words, which tells me how many words I can use explaining each concept, which in turn helps me decide where I can slow down and explain things, and where I need to limit my personal quest to include all of the details.

This can lead to some agonizing decisions, too. In many ways, writing a children's book is extremely formulaic, because you must be equal parts meaningful and concise; a teacher and an usher; an educator and an entertainer.

It's not easy. I can't tell you how many scenes or pages I've written for a Young Adult book, only to realize I just spent ¾ of my chapter explaining one concept and now have no room for plot development. I honestly find this part agonizing. I sigh deeply and my hand quivers as I highlight the text I've just laboriously typed, wincing in pain as I tap Control and the X key simultaneously. And that's why I have a file on my computer dedicated to "Deleted Scenes."

However, where there is agony, there is also ecstasy. The thrill of figuring out exactly the right words to fully express your idea without hijacking your entire book is akin to working a particularly difficult jigsaw, crossword, or logic puzzle, or finding the right spice that takes your recipe to the next level—it feels the same way we want our readers to feel when they encounter those words for the first time.

You will likely need to fidget with your pacing as you start writing your children's book, especially if you've had lots of practice writing for adults.

I have a little exercise for this that I call "How We Got There." Essentially I write one sentence as the beginning of the scene. Let's say:

Waldo ate eggs for breakfast on Wednesday morning.

Now, write another sentence that doesn't seem to relate at first:

Waldo was happy to have new tap dancing shoes today.

If you aren't feeling up to creating your own first and last sentences, or you want an especially challenging practice session, grab two sentences from any random news story.

From here, you just need to fill in the details to make an entire story:

Waldo ate eggs for breakfast on Wednesday morning. He was nervous, because he had dance class that afternoon. His class was learning a new tap dance. Last week, Waldo's tap shoe had broken during class, and he slipped and fell. Waldo was happy to have new tap dancing shoes today, but still a little nervous. What if the other kids made fun of him about his fall?

While this is just a practice example, and you can use as many words as you want when figuring out your own tale, I encourage you to consider thinking about how this would fit in an actual child's book.

Look at your text and compare it to the spatial confines of the actual book you would write. Does it seem like a lot? Does it seem like too little? How many inches of page space can you actually give to Waldo, his eggs, and his tap shoes?

Furthermore, how much of this information is necessary? Do we need to know about the new tap dance at all, or would it help the audience to know what kind of move caused Waldo's mishap? Why are the eggs mentioned at all... or should we be asking whether they're scrambled or over-hard?

At this point you might be wondering why we mentioned Waldo at all, if all we end up with is more unanswerable questions. In fact, the unanswerable questions are the entire point of the exercise.

There are innumerable ways to get from Point A to Point B in a story. None of them are necessarily wrong or bad paths to take; in fact, every possible writing path you could take will have its own advantages, disadvantages, and challenges. You might come up too short and leave your audience with just as many unanswerable questions. You might go too quickly for your readers and lose their attention because they simply don't understand. But just as risky is drawing things out too much and boring them with too much detail.

Therein lies the rub, and hence why some novice children's authors throw their hands up and abandon their project before their self-confidence completely tanks.

Getting the right pace and finding the right words can be a difficult journey wrought with self-doubt. Ultimately, however, this is another instance in which practice is the only way to really get a feel for the art of the perfect pace. Therefore, I encourage you to consider each sentence you write as another opportunity for practice, not another shot at perfection. If there actually was a "perfect" book, none of us would bother writing at all, and yet here we are.

Exercises such as this little journey with Waldo here can help you get a feel for where your voice tends to drift. I tend to go long format and would happily tell you about every emotional and physical ache and pain Waldo had experienced since his fall. By doing exercises like this, however, I have learned to rein myself in more and more, carefully adding this detail here and that detail there to enhance the reader's overall understanding without overwhelming them to concepts.

I stated that the process feels more like "building" a book than writing one. To loop this back to architecture, think of a young child's drawing of a house versus the in-person appearance of an ornate Victorian manor. The first will display just the basic functional suggestion of a house, usually in one-dimensional splendor. The latter will provide an almost overwhelming array of turrets, gables, stained glass, corbels, and trim, not to mention a color palette of many bold, contrasting colors.

The book you are building will likely share aspects of each home design. The balance between the two, however, is something that lies within you and can be refined through (infinite) practice.

Insight into Kids and Books : Show Vs. Tell

Note: This section deals with the concepts of using pictures versus creating a picture with words that young readers can appreciate. This is not intended to discriminate against youngsters working with sight impairment issues. I'm afraid I don't have much experience in writing specifically for blind/low vision children, but I understand great advances are being made in the field of tactile picture books as well as beginner Braille books.

Another thing we have to keep in mind as children's book authors is that we can also rely on actual pictures to help out with the whole "worth 1000 words" thing. What better way to demonstrate an idea than by actually showing an unfamiliar audience member the very thing you're trying to describe?

For readers under a certain age, pictures of some sort are absolutely necessary. Imagine a picture book without pictures. A page stares at you with no emotion. "Look at the cat," the page reads. But there is no cat to look at, just the four-word command before you.

As we've discussed, the point of pictures in a book is to illustrate a concept. If you've ever taken a course in microbiology, for example, your textbooks were likely filled with pictures of all sorts of magnified views of specimens, diagrams of cells, and charts and graphs of all sorts.

But those illustrations were for educational purposes only and only contained flamboyant colors or decorative flair by accident. The pictures we put into a children's book have to be attractive and entertaining in addition to being educational. In other words, not just any old picture will do.

Typically we use illustrations and photos to help children visualize and comprehend the scene that is taking place within the words. Illustrations are drawings, paintings, or other hand-created renderings, while photos are actual photographs of existing things. Thanks to AI and photo editing tools, there can be some overlap between the two.

Deciding on how you want to present your visuals can be a pretty involved process. You'll need to consider:

- Basic formatting, such as page size, illustration to text ratio, number of pages, and number of pictures.

- What type of visuals you want—examples can include full color detailed scene drawings, small black-and-white thumbnails to accompany the text, full page artistic interpretations, or diagrams.

- Design elements, such as the style, color palette used, mood, and artistic theme. You want the visual aspects of the book to emphasize and enhance your text, not overpower or underwhelm it.

But perhaps most importantly, you'll need to decide where you're getting these pictures. If you happen to be artistically inclined, then this is a short-lived quest, limited only by your ability to produce visual art and written pieces simultaneously. After all, we only have so many hands.

If you are not artistically inclined, or recognize that trying to do your characters justice will leave you feeling more frustrated than elated, there are ways to source art. There are plenty of artists, photographers, illustrators, cartoonists, graphic artists, and other creators who would absolutely love to help you with your project. There's just one catch: you need to pay them.

Being successful as a creative type does hinge greatly on the right person seeing your work at exactly the right time, so I like to think that those who offer me lengthy, difficult jobs for little or no pay have their hearts in the right place when they say things like, "but think of the exposure!" Unfortunately, my cell phone provider has absolutely no interest in reading any of my books, and my bank doesn't accept a print out of the comment section of an article in which I'm complimented as payment for my mortgage. Exposure is important, but so is eating, and that requires actual money.

Therefore, you have to keep in mind how many pictures you can afford to source for your children's book. While you're at it, you may also want to determine what type of visuals you can add to your book in the first place. Whether you're self-publishing or sending the draft out in hopes of getting a big-name contract, you'll need to be aware of each party's rules about the file type, size, and number of pictures that can be added, along with specific requirements on giving credit for artwork. It's a good idea to know what you are fully capable of doing before you start hiring artists and commissioning artwork.

Depending on your overall artistic vision, it may be a good idea to consider your artistic budget early in the planning process. While it is equally true that "a picture says a thousand words" and "authors paint pictures with words," the small size and concise package of a children's book means that authors need to make deliberate choices in both words and pictures.

For most writers, the hardest part is putting the words together to make a book. This seems somewhat obvious, but it's a little deeper than choosing the right word to describe a particular shade of red or the fluffiness of a dog.

Each word an author writes is a part of the whole book. Each word matters. When we're writing casually for other adults, we don't often actively consider this. Marketing and advertising specialists are actively aware of how words work on a psychological and emotional level, but most of us write with the intention of sharing information.

When we choose to write a book, we move beyond basic information sharing. This isn't an email to Payroll to advise of upcoming time off. This is an opportunity to reach out and touch the brains and hearts of readers. You can ignite emotions, reveal new information, and provide life-changing details all by arranging some words on a page.

And when you choose to write a book for children, the challenge is even greater. The stakes are higher, with an audience who needs greater engagement, and who may have never encountered the words with which you've written your book. Finding just the right words to grab their attention, to entertain them, to educate them, and to create a lasting memory in their lives? It seems impossible, but struggling through practice to get just the right message in front of just the right child is absolutely worth it.

Chapter Three

Creating a World Specifically for Children

Now that we've talked at great length about the mechanics and format of children's literature, it's time to dive into some of the less obvious things that differentiate a children's book from one intended for an adult audience.

I know we've talked at length about the importance of shedding our adult perspectives, and how it's important to use words and situations that are familiar to your audience. We've considered how our overall writing style can be adapted to be more child-friendly, as well. Now it's time to take a look at your voice, your characters, and how your message is conveyed to the reader.

You may have noticed that we've been getting progressively subjective in subject matter as these chapters continue. Vocabulary lists and the size and shape of a book can be objectively measured and weighed against common logic. Ostensibly, a toddler's picture book won't be a 100-page multisyllabic odyssey, while a book intended for high schoolers will land flat if it's too simple.

But once we step past the simple mechanics of a book and into the art of language, things become a little less obvious. The last section of this book may seem like a disjointed flowchart of if/then statements and possibilities.

And truly, the experience of writing a children's book can be a little gelatinous, or even vapory. As grown adults with what we hope is a greater-than-average knowledge of our native language, it is all too easy to approach a task like a children's book with a certain naivete and ego. *What could possibly be so hard about writing a simple children's book? How stressful can it be to slap together 20 pages of text and pictures? People have made longer PowerPoint presentations in less than an hour!* And yet, when we actually sit down to make it happen, we realize that there are a lot more moving pieces than we probably thought. All of our best intentions evaporate. We struggle with language. The picture we formed of our perfect children's book starts to fade.

Consider the previous section a sort of safety net to catch all of those moving places as they struggle to wriggle just out of your grasp. You are now aware that you've got to pay close attention to which words you use, where you put them, how many of them you use, and how rapidly you'll want to fire them at your reader. You've got the tools to build your own sort of gridwork to keep these elements from slipping too far out of your line of sight by nailing them to an orderly page fashion. You're on the right path, and even though it may seem like some new challenge is awaiting beyond every comma, you're heading forward.

But there's one thing that I feel really and truly brings a children's book together. Children, I believe, are more acutely aware of something that adults often forget: that there's a human on the other side of the book.

As adults, we tend to take our narrators and characters for granted. Within a few pages of reading any text, we can tell whether or not we like, trust, or even want to listen to the voice that is bringing us this data. And we are blissfully unaware of it.

Can you think of an advertisement or commercial that you just can't stand? Maybe there's an ad that shows up on your favorite blog that just makes you question why you visit the site in the first place. Or perhaps you've seen a television commercial that irks you to the point of wanting to boycott the entire brand. These are not unusual reactions; in fact, they're proof that words have both intellectual and psychological weight. We react not only to the words that are present-ed and the concepts they represent, but how they are presented and if we feel comfortable with the manner in which they're presented.

Therefore, tone, voice, and establishing characters who are relatable and sympathetic can help readers get the most out of your book. Think about that ad or commercial you don't like. Focus specifically on the delivery of the message—the characters, any voiceovers, and text incorporated into the ad. What is it that irks you? How could this message have been delivered in a way that evokes a more positive response for you?

Consider that a television advertisement lasts about 15-30 seconds, and a print ad is only in front of your face as long as you choose to look at it. Suddenly, that 20-page Powerpoint presentation of a children's book seems a little more serious, doesn't it?

But not impossible. Let's take a look at how the storytelling process itself can help you create a book that you can enjoy writing just as much as the young readers will enjoy flipping through the pages some day!

The Importance of the Narrator

No matter what your book is about, who it's geared toward, or how many words it has, the story has to be told by someone.

The role of this narrator is very basic in the early years. Simple identifying phrases for picture books, like "A is for Apple" or "The apple is red," don't have the same opportunity to be as engaging as the narrator of a chapter book, for example.

Which brings us to a really big question: what is engagement, and how do you create it?

I think most passionate readers—regardless of age—would emphatically state that there is no one factor that drives reader engagement. It's not the same for every reader, and it's not the same for every book. That's why there are so many books in the world in the first place—we all love different stuff.

I believe that writing an engaging book is somewhat like working with a new recipe in the kitchen. You can swear up and down that you did the exact same thing each time, but each batch- or in this case, book- turns out a little differently. That is, of course, until you've had enough practice and developed the stamina to boldly move from step to step (or word to word) without fear of failure and the confidence that you can correct any error that comes your way.

Your narrator, whoever it is, is at the heart of the recipe, keeping all of the moving pieces and parts together. The narrator is the gravy in the stew, the sauce in the pasta, and the milk in the roux. Your narrator is a major driving force behind your book being engaging.

In previous books I've referred to an exercise I call "Narrate Your Day," in which you warm up your writing brain by simply narrating what you're doing, as you do it. For example:

"She continued typing the sentence, occasionally striking the wrong key, cursing and pausing to sip her apple-honey tea before correcting the error. It was no wonder she kept losing her train of thought, she chided herself. Still, the tea was delicious, the local honey supported farmers in her community, and she reminded herself that hydration and small treats are important for your overall health."

In this context, however, we're writing for children, so consider adjusting the exercise to narrate your day through the lens of a child. Using the same scene as above:

"She kept typing and typing. Every now and then something went wrong. It was easy to tell because she would stop typing and loudly say some adult words. Then she would take a sip of tea and start typing again like nothing had happened."

At first, switching the perspective may feel super awkward. Reading over my example, I feel like I could do much better. However, I'm leaving that as is because that was my first attempt. Your first attempt at narrating from a child's perspective may be equally dissatisfying. But here's the absolutely wonderful thing about writing exercises—you can keep doing them, playing and practicing with your words, until you feel satisfied with the result. What if I changed it a bit:

"She drank a lot of tea. She said it kept her calm, but the only time she drank it was when she made a mistake in her typing. Then she yelled bad words and drank a lot of tea."

When you're starting a new book, it may take some time before you really get to know your narrator. But first, you have to decide who your narrator is, which means choosing from a few conventional options.

The Narrator Who Is Everywhere at Once

In children's books, this is often a nameless, faceless, highly subjective, omniscient, omnipresent being who is able to accurately report on events occurring at all sorts of times and places—sometimes even simultaneously.

Young readers can tell that *someone* is telling this story, but they're not necessarily worried about who that is or why they know everyone's thoughts and feelings, as long as we're fully immersed in the story. And as long as this invisible narrator keeps explaining everything to the audience in a way that makes them want to know more, immersion is an achievable goal.

Using a third person omniscient voice tends to be a popular choice for young reader narratives because of this fact. Suspension of disbelief is much easier when you're very young and anything seems possible. Somehow, young readers don't feel the need to question how just one person could possibly know what the Velveteen Rabbit was thinking, *and* how the real rabbits made fun of him, *and* the Skin Horse's backstory, *and* where the nursery magic Fairy took him at the end.

As a writer, you can limit how much omniscience your narrator really has. Maybe the reader has direct insight into how the main character and her best friend are feeling and what they're thinking, but we have no idea how the main character's mom is going to react, or what's going to happen Monday at school.

I like to think of this type of narrator as the camera perspective in most movies or television shows. In real life, we would have no idea what was going on in two characters' apartments located across town from each other. But thanks to the omniscient third person narrator, we can observe both sides of a telephone conversation, appreciate how each participant feels during a first date, or know which character is getting grounded before they even get home from their mischievous deeds. Just as a camera cuts from one scene to the next, a turn of the page can transport us across space and time and into another character's experience.

In my "Narrate Your Day" example earlier, I used this type of narrator for both the adult and child examples. We get the impression that we are observing this furiously typing fool from a distance; however, we also know the reasoning behind her actions. We have both "inside" information or invisible details, such as thoughts, emotions, prior experiences, opinions, as well as "outside" information or observable details, including what the character is doing and saying.

You may also note the simplified view the narrator takes in the children's books examples versus the adult version. The narrator limits how much insight they share based on the audience. Many adults are familiar with coming up with reasons why indulging in a treat is perfectly reasonable. Taking too many tea breaks when you're supposed to be meeting a deadline can be a problem; however, it is not a child's problem. Children would have a limited idea of why the origin of the honey in the tea would make it a good excuse for not getting work done.

As any good chef knows, the ingredients of a dish must satisfy the palate of the person who will consume it; therefore, just as you might tone down the spice or complexity of a sauce for children, you might need to whittle down how much you share with your young audience. Spend some time getting to know your third person omniscient narrator through writing exercises as you get started, and you may find that it's a little easier to take on their perspective.

The Ever-Tricky First Person

As readers gain experience, first person narratives become more commonplace on the bookshelves. Telling a story through the eyes of a main character can really ramp up engagement with readers who can appreciate a different perspective. Just the subtle shift from "Jim and Vaughn went to the store" to "Jim and I went to the store" removes the reader from watching the story unfold from an observer's seat to actually being a part of the action. However, while a first person narrator can be extremely engaging for young readers, there are plenty of ways in which it can be troublesome for the adult author.

The biggest obstacle—in my humble opinion—is the whole "adult" thing. If you're going to write from the point of view of a child, it actually has to sound like a child's point of view. All of the things mentioned earlier about vocabulary and a child's level of emotional understanding and experience? They really come in handy here. Kids will be able to pick up on the fact that Vaughn the 10-year-old from New Jersey sounds a lot more like their 35-year-old aunt from the suburban Midwest— unless you actually do your best to write in the voice of a 10-year-old from New Jersey. We'll talk about voice more in the next section, but keep this in mind as you consider whether a first person narrative is right for your book.

When writing a story from a first-person perspective, you also have the ability to really dive into that character's emotions, thoughts, and observations. In fact, you can write pages upon pages of emotive text as you personally explore what your characters are going through. Here you encounter two distinct dilemmas we've already discussed: not only have you used valuable page space ignoring the plot, but you might be exhausting the emotional capacity of your reader.

It can be blissfully cathartic to use your first person narrator to work through your own childhood experience. I once wrote a character who was experiencing bullying because she's chubby. This is a very common childhood situation; so common, in fact, that I have volumes of personal anecdotes to draw from for inspiration.

Somewhere along the lines, I found myself writing a really long scene in which our heroine is bullied in math class. As I typed, I cried. I processed a whole slew of similar scenes from my own younger days as I followed this particular scene through in my head. It was the most poignant writing of my career—and no one has read it. Once I finished it, I realized it put the chapter a whopping 4,000 words over my chapter limit, based on my initial framework. So I did what any responsible writer would do—I highlighted that section, cut it from the manuscript, and pasted it in a separate document I have set aside for such occasions.

The compact nature of children's books can make it difficult for us to fully capture our very complicated adult understanding of emotions. And as we guide our first person narrator through their journey, we may find ourselves pausing to reflect more than the constraints of a page limit allow. This is where your grid can help stay on track with moving your plot forward, developing your characters' voices, and avoiding trauma dumping on a young audience.

Ultimately, the challenge of limiting your first person narrator is the same as reining in your third person omniscient narrator—sure, you know absolutely everything there is to know, but the amount you share and how you share it has to be kid-friendly and more importantly, kid-engaging.

So how do we practice our first person narrative? For me, the answer isn't too far away from the "Narrate Your Day" exercise. I call this one "Dear Journal," because it feels a lot like journaling, without the deep introspection.

At the end of the day, once my list of verbs has dwindled to "pull up the covers" and "go to sleep," I consider what happened while I was awake:

I woke up with a big, fluffy kitty on my chest. The world was dark on the other side of my bedroom curtains. I wished that Polly's breakfast time and my sleeping schedule were the same, just once.

After making Polly's wishes come true, showering, and brushing my teeth, it seemed like a good idea to get the day started. I plopped down into my rolling desk chair, causing it to scoot just far enough away from my desk that I couldn't reach the keyboard. "Great," I thought to myself. "It's going to be that kind of day."

It's not dissimilar to journaling, but with the intention of writing for an audience. Perhaps this is why I have such a rough time journaling– I'm far more familiar with writing for others than I am for myself!

To that point, don't do this exercise– or any other– to your detriment, but rather to help you organize the process of where your creative brain needs to go in order to help you express your ideas.

Practice doesn't necessarily make perfect, after all– but it does improve overall patience. And patience is a very helpful tool for those who plan to build a children's book.

All About You, The Second Person

If you truly love a challenge, there's always a second person narrative. In this case, the reader is the narrator:

You wake up with a big, fluffy kitty on your chest. The world is dark on the other side of your bedroom curtains. You wish Polly's breakfast time and your sleeping schedule were the same, just once.

After making Polly's wishes come true, showering, and brushing your teeth, it seemed like a good idea to get the day started. You plopped down into your rolling desk chair, causing it to scoot just far enough away from your desk that you couldn't reach the keyboard. "Great," you think to yourself. "It's going to be that kind of day."

Second person is very much a valid narrative style, but it's also one of the most divisive. Some readers feel that reading from the "you" perspective makes the experience incredibly personal. Others feel that being told how you're feeling and what you're thinking is overly distracting.

It is true that in a second person narrative, you are receiving direct information about what you are feeling and thinking– in the sense that you *are*, in fact, the main character of this tale. No one is telling you how to feel and think as a reader.

At the same time, it is quite possible that your own response to the situations the main character endures are very different. It can be challenging for some readers to reconcile what they're being told they feel with what they actually feel.

Then again, certain young audiences may appreciate the second person approach as a way to help them understand how to navigate new and scary situations. A second person book about the first day of school, for example, might help relieve some pre-kindergarten jitters:

Today you are taking the bus for the first time. Mommy walks with you to the place where the bus will pick you up. There are one, two, three, four other kids there with their mommies and daddies. It is their first time riding the bus, too. All four kids have a scared look on their face. One boy has red puffy cheeks like he had been crying. You remember how Mommy said most kids are nervous about the first day of school, just like you are. You wonder if they have butterflies flip-flopping in their tummies, too.

The second person is more immersive; however, you have to be careful exactly how immersive you get. It's entirely possible to influence a young mind to associate feelings with a situation, even if they didn't really feel that way to begin with. A child who feels totally confident about the first day of school might question their attitude after reading the example above, while a child who is experiencing anxiety will feel comforted and more secure.

So how do you write a book about the first day of school that both confident and anxious children can relate to? While there are several ways to solve this problem, the most basic options are:

1. Write from a neutral standpoint that acknowledges all potential perspectives

2. Don't try to please everyone, and choose the perspective that most relates to the book you want to write

This is not exclusive to second-person narratives, of course. No matter what book you write, you will not please every child, parent, teacher, and children's librarian in the world. However, you can provide them with appropriate and sincere guidance as to the content that lies in between your book's covers. There are several ways to do this:

- Full disclosure book descriptions: "This second person narrative explores feeling scared about the first day of school so nervous children feel less alone in their anxiety."

- Very clear opening sequences: "Today is your first day of school. You are excited to meet new friends. You are also scared. What if the other kids don't like you? What if you do something wrong?"

- Strong book titles: "First Day of School Fears" or "How the
  Scary First Day Became the Best Day Ever"

Also– and I say this with all kindness in my heart– no one will ever be fully prepared for the impact your book has on them. The wisdom of our ancestors states that it is unwise to judge a book by its cover, after all.

Ultimately, if you feel comfortable experimenting in second person, you should absolutely give it a whirl. I obviously am not entirely comfortable in this format, but I encourage you to seek out examples from authors who do an exceptional job, including *I Am Golden* by Eva Chen and Sophie Diao, *Do Not Bring Your Dragon to the Library* by Julie Gassman, and *The Iridescence of Birds: A Book About Henri Matisse* by Patricia MacLachlan and Hadley Hooper.

The Kind Authority

Lest non-fiction writers believe I've forgotten them, allow me to introduce the type of perspective I call "The Kind Authority." Since non-fiction books aren't narratives, there is no narrator, per se, but that doesn't mean that these books should be devoid of any sort of voice. However, whenever we put words to a page, it is inevitable that they should have personality and style.

The Authority doesn't necessarily have to be "kind." Furthermore, I don't use the term "kind" to suggest that you might actually choose to use The Rude Authority perspective. Instead, I refer to the rather genial role that educators who are also entertaining tend to play. Think of popular children's figures like Mr. Rogers, Blippi, Shari Lewis, and Bill Nye.

Presenting brand new facts to young minds isn't challenging simply because of the delicate process of introducing fresh realities—you also have to do so in a way that delights them and encourages curiosity. Your Kind Authority has the ability to make that happen.

With your text, you have the potential for turning what adults consider "common knowledge" into a mind-blowing realization for a youngster.

And while it's hard to capture the attention of an adult without tip-toeing into hyperbole, kids are frequently mesmerized by relatable comparisons. Once, I entertained my niece for almost an entire hour by explaining how tall different animals are compared to her dog. My friend has a horse that is about three Mochas tall. My huge cat is about half of a Mocha. A giraffe is about five Mochas just from the ground to the base of the neck.

While you can't possibly know how big each dog in your audience might be, consider this example when attempting to provide units of measurement or comparisons. We've discussed this concept in terms of the words you use, but think about the manner in which you present this information.

Consider a little exercise I like to call "Make It Interesting, Not Longer." I'm sure this won't come as a shock to anyone, but I tend to the verbose. Kids aren't into this. I also revel in the opportunity to wander into an obtuse level of detail when explaining something. Many children actively hate this.

To prevent myself from taking a young audience on a side quest they neither requested nor deserve, I try to create a partnership between the simplest version of a fact and a sympathetic, easy-to-follow instruction, without taking up too much page space trying to be interesting. To be completely honest, this is the part that makes me the most nervous. I've enjoyed loquacious prattling since I learned the meaning of each word, so this is exceptionally difficult for me.

However, this exercise helps me tone it down for children's books by forcing me to focus on what I actually want to deliver.

The first thing I do is simplify my facts to the most basic elements, as we did in the earlier exercise. For the purpose of practicing, this can be any basic fact. I recommend choosing a topic that really holds your attention so you don't grow bored or frustrated and give up. There have been times when my passion for a book topic has been the only thing pressing me through the emotionally trying times, so set yourself up for success when practicing.

As for my example, let's say I'm writing a biography about Fred Rogers. My most simplified version would be something along the lines of:

Fred Rogers used his imagination to create a world known as Mr. Rogers' Neighborhood. This world became a television show. On his show, Mr. Rogers used puppets and songs to teach children about the world around them.

All of that is true, but it's also boring. None of that captures the Henrietta Pussycat voice, or the time Mr. Rogers quietly explained to all of us that segregation was wrong with a simple kiddy pool.

So let's make it a little more interesting:

With the ding of a trolley bell and a song that everyone knew, children were able to visit Mr. Rogers' Neighborhood for 33 years thanks to television. Fred Rogers was a trained musician who made up songs and skits for his puppet characters. He liked to talk about things like feelings and dealing with problems.

Too much? It is 18 words longer. What about this:

Thanks to public television, children could hop aboard the Neighborhood Trolley and visit Mr. Roger's Neighborhood. Fred Rogers was a trained musician who made up songs and skits for his puppet characters. He liked to talk about things like feelings and dealing with problems.

You can continue massaging your own exercise forever, but ultimately, you'll find yourself with a version you actually like quite a bit. And in many cases, if you write your next fact with the same intentions, and then the next fact, and the one after that, you'll likely get into a groove that we like to call "finding your voice."

And that is how the Kind Authority is often conceived and born. Each author's Kind Authority voice will sound different, much as our actual physical voices are unique. With practice, your Kind Authority might just sound more informative and confident than the real-life you!

Notes about Finding the Right Tone and Voice

In each of these examples, I've made reference to "getting to know your narrator." By that, I don't mean that you really need to sit down and consider the whole raison d'être for your narrator and their place within the metaverse of your book—you can, but I don't know that Dr. Seuss really went cosmically deep for *Hop on Pop*. Instead, I encourage you to become acquainted with your narrator's tone and voice.

I find that the narrator's style in a children's book—whether first or third person—often takes on one of two personas: The Story Teller or The Explainer.

I consider The Story Teller a narrator who wants to move the story forward as much as possible. Just like a person telling another person a story, this narrator is detailed and personable, but mostly linear in their approach of the tale. One event leads into another with minimal backtracking or backstories, but the reader has a full sensory and emotional understanding of each scene and character. The Story Teller's goal is to immerse the reader in a new world and take them through this amazing adventure.

The Explainer, on the other hand, is very much interested in sharing the whys and hows of the plot and character activity. This type of narrator might go into the details of why a certain character has a phrase they repeat frequently, or take us on the entire path to show us how a character gets home after school. These might not be terribly deep insights, but The Explainer wants to make sure that readers really understand everything that's happening.

In conversation, many of us naturally shift between these two voices. That being said, very few of us consistently make that shift well. Have you ever been conversing with a friend and realized that you've probably gone a little deeper into the background explanation of a topic than you needed to? Perhaps they have a mildly con-fused, glazed-over look that tells you that they are no longer following. Maybe they've started fidgeting, or they're glancing around furtively for something to distract them from your detailed rambling. All of these are signs that your inner Explainer has made things awk-ward—albeit with the best intentions, of course.

Unfortunately, you can't always be present to see if your young audience reacts the same way. That means you (and your editors/beta readers, if you have them) will have to moderate The Explainer.

This is not so much something you can practice with exercises so much as through self-awareness. Many of us creative types struggle with self-awareness as we're getting started with our writing, however. It's completely natural. Just as we considered how children are new to this whole "world" thing, you are new to this whole "writing" thing. Give yourself grace and let yourself naturally develop an understand-ing of your style, voice, and tone, and take your time considering how you can improve. Keep trying something a little different until you finally read what's on the page and loudly exclaim, "Yes! That's what I've been trying to say this entire time!"

To curb The Explainer, I encourage you to start by re-reading what you've written. This may seem like an obvious part of the writing process, but in this case, don't read what you just wrote—look at what you wrote several days ago, or last week.

Choose a passage where you had to be an Agent of Discovery and introduce a new topic to your readers. Give it a nice, thorough read. Then ask yourself:

- How was it, overall?

- Did it tell your reader everything they needed to know about the concept?

- Are they prepared for the rest of the book with the information they received?

- Do you want to know more about that concept after reading this passage?

- Is there any way to insert an explanation without actually explaining?

Helpful hint: this is a great place to practice using your context. Try to focus more on how your narrator would explain this concept instead of how you personally would educate others on the matter. By hiding clarifications and definitions in the narration, you're essentially hiding vegetables in the stew—instead of forcing new ideas down your readers' throats, you're presenting them in easy-to-digest, fully tangible ways that make learning new things seem downright yummy.

Relatable Characters Have a Guiding Role

There are very few hard and fast rules when it comes to writing books. After all, creative types don't really enjoy being told not to do something—we just come up with a new form of artistic subversion.

That being said, if you choose to write a fiction book for children, you really need at least one major character who is the same age as the prospective audience members.

The reason for this is because you are trying to connect with an audience who has a specific point of view. They have certain priorities in life and an ever-developing knowledge base that occasionally adjusts these priorities. At some point in life, saving your allowance money for a big treat becomes more important than spending it all right away on a favorite candy, for example.

Young readers will look for something they recognize in your text. If they can't relate to any of the characters, then why on Earth would they want to waste their time forcing themselves to read your book? With the exception of required reading for school, most young readers will discard a book that is boring and devour one that draws them in. Your cast of characters can not only invite your young reader into the tale, but warmly welcome them along on the journey.

There's one important part of characterization and point of view that we often neglect—the experience of interaction.

Even as adults, we act differently in the presence of authority figures. You may beg to differ, but if you've ever found yourself easing off the accelerator and turning down the music when a police car joins traffic, I'm afraid you're just as susceptible to this phenomenon as the rest of us.

The difference between adults and children is that to children, everyone is an authority figure. In a child's eyes, the 16-year-old babysitter is an authority. Technically your older sibling is an author-ity figure, but one that you actively challenge. Your siblings' friends and your friends' siblings are kind of a grey area, but they tend to have your best interest in mind. Parents are to be respected—especially other kids' parents. Your parents' friends are on that tier as well, re-gardless of whether they have kids or not. Teachers, doctors, religious leaders, and expert adults are essentially top-tier authority from a kid's perspective, so the way they interact with these individuals is totally different.

These rules are, of course, not all-inclusive, but simply meant to demonstrate how the hierarchy of power in a children's book may be a bit tricky for us to recall and reconstruct as grown adults. Your reader expects certain types of interactions between characters in order to really lean into their relatability.

So what exactly does that mean? Things like calling adults by an approved name, like "Mrs. K" or "Dr. Gaiter" provide that realism in interaction. Having a young character feel a little nervous in the principal's office, even if they've done nothing wrong, can help a child tune in to similarities between themselves and your characters.

Emotions and sensory experiences tend to coax children into relat-ing further to characters. Interestingly enough, while adults tend to relate more to very specific descriptors, children can do with far less. For example:

"Mrs. Donahue smelled just like my grandma."

As an adult reader, you want to know exactly what that means. There are several distinct grandmotherly scent profiles. Is this more Avon perfume and potpourri, or vitamins and antiseptic spray? Chocolate chip cookies and really old furniture? Was Grandma a professional diesel mechanic? My adult mind really needs to know.

But a child will likely fill in the gaps with what they know to be the official scent of grandmothers. In their limited experience, there are typically only one or two ways a grandmother can smell. On top of that, the smell is typically informed by experiences associated with that individual, rather than their actual smell. Grammy smells like McDonald's and an old change purse because your family used to meet her there for breakfast every other Saturday, and she always bought coffee and a hashbrown with change from that purse. In reality, she might have smelled entirely different, but as a child, your impression of her has been formed around this specific, memorable situation.

But there's also the chance that the reader has no idea what potpourri or McDonald's coffee smells like. These aren't necessarily universal experiences for children. Therefore, while the temptation to be specific is strong, there are times when being vague will help children connect further with a character.

So what makes a character relatable? Furthermore, why do we need a relatable character? Ultimately, a young reader will relate most to a character who shares their point of view, who experiences similar interactions, and who shares an intimate knowledge of the world around them. As a result, a character in the same age group is considered a must.

Imagine if the Hunger Games recruited adults from each district, rather than a child. The pressures and conflict Katniss Everdeen feels as a volunteer tribute when her younger sister's name is called are only relatable to a younger audience because Katniss is herself a child. And while the circumstances of sacrificing your entire life for your sister is hopefully not directly relatable, many young adult readers probably appreciate how hard it is to balance so many different emotions that seem to have life-or-death consequences as a teenager.

Kids appreciate reading about kids because they experience similar situations. Kids don't know what it's like to try to finance a motorcycle, but many of them understand what it's like to try to ride a bike for the first time. A reader who can fall in stride with a leading character will settle into the story much faster and with greater comfort. As an author, you get to choose exactly what tools and techniques you use to create that relatability.

When Your Characters Aren't Really People

There is one way to somewhat get around this requirement: anthropomorphism. Winnie the Pooh and friends created by A. A. Milne , Harold and Chester from the *Bunnicula* series by James Howe and Deborah Howe, and the main characters of Thomas M. Disch's *The Brave Little Toaster* are all examples of non-human entities that behave in very human ways. They have conversations, share their thoughts, come up with plans, have ideas, and interact with each other in a manner that is almost exactly like our own human experience.

I say "almost" because it is important to at least somewhat distinguish your characters who are sentient toys, animals, or kitchen appliances from the human characters. While Christopher Robin interacts with Pooh and his crew, they typically do so within the expansive imaginary world of The Hundred Acre Wood. Harold and Chester interact with humans and each other exactly as you would imagine a dog and cat doing in real life—grooming themselves, making messes, and being confused at human antics. The appliances in *The Brave Little Toaster* specifically mention that they must be perfectly still whenever humans are around.

There are, of course, exceptions—Pete the Cat doesn't have any human friends in the original book series. Pete the Cat is also known for short picture book adventures suitable for readers aged 3-7 and board books for even younger audiences. A simpler book often requires a more basic world of characters and settings in which an undemanding plot is developed in a straightforward manner, as we've collectively considered several times so far.

So, using a non-human character to connect to your audience is very possible, but it can also be tricky. You'll need to invent the rules for how these things co-exist with humans— if they co-exist with humans—as well as the context of their world. Which objects/animals are sentient? Do they all speak the same language? Can they understand humans? Can humans understand them? Can they interact with humans? Can they interact with each other—for example, can my cat and my dishwasher have a conversation?

All of these things are possible—after all, it is your book. But whereas in a human world we have social structure and roles, you'll need to figure out how these ideas translate into your fictional world. Who is the primary authority in the bathroom—the toilet or the sink?— for example.

On top of that, you will still need a sympathetic character for your readers. Whether your sentient objects have the mental and developmental level of your readers or they interact with humans in the right age group, there still needs to be a relatable anchor to the tale. After all, the Velveteen Rabbit would've never become real if there hadn't been a little boy to love him.

Whether you choose a first person narrator who is a member of your target demographic, an omniscient narrator with a cast of young characters, or give the power of speech to the draperies, don't forget that the characters in your book not only have to work to move the plot of your book along, and help develop the mood and explore the emotional implications of the events of the book all while informing and entertaining the reader—they also need to carefully usher the young reader through each page turn of the book with their relatability.

This sounds like a lot, but if you think about it for a moment, all of these things are inextricably linked.

Your Characters, Their Emotions, and Your Reader

Characters, much like humans, are essentially a bunch of actions and reactions. Some of those may be physical reactions, while others may be emotional or mental. A simple conversation between characters can display all of the above.

But unless you are writing some sort of absurdist literature for children, there will be emotion in your book. There will be personality. There will be some form of personal expression. Even Dick and Jane had fun.

So as you think of things like *inter*actions between your characters, keep in mind the *re*actions of your characters, as well.

For a child, nearly everything has the ability to be a plot twist. Moving or changing schools, parents getting divorced, losing a pet, or having a strict teacher can be huge emotional triggers for children. At the same time, some of the things we find horrendous as adults, like war, disease, and criminal activity, aren't necessarily as serious for children.

The reason for this disparity starts with the fact that children are new to this. All of this. As previously mentioned, they don't have a basis for understanding more complex things. Therefore, things that directly impact the way they experience everyday living are very real and terrifying threats.

Children have a lesser understanding about large-scale suffering because in many ways, it's too big to understand. They might memorize the fact that thousands of people died in a conflict, but they probably don't even know thousands of people in real life. Outside of a sports stadium or other such crowded event, they might not have a concept of how many people that really might be. On an emotional level, they don't necessarily feel as terrible about thousands of people they've never met or known disappearing from the Earth, because those people simply never existed in their reality and the concept simply doesn't register.

Over time and with more experience as human beings, we become more empathetic with the facts of life and the human condition. By the time readers get to *The Diary of a Young Girl* by Anne Frank, their understanding of why these events are so horrific is solidified by reading a first person perspective of the impact they had, as they are occurring to the young author.

So when your character reacts to something terrible happening in their life, think not about how you would react, but how your character would react. This is standard procedure for any fiction writer, but when you're writing for children, there's that whole pesky perspective difference. While you, the adult reading this book, might have a tense emotional response every time you glance at the news, a child may shrug and ask to go play instead of watching the broadcast of fresh new horrors.

This is another instance in which having eyes on the ground in the juvenile community can be helpful. Just as I suggested consulting with children about their reactions to heavy topics, you might want to consider how they deal with big emotions. Do they talk to their friends? Do they look up information to learn more about what's bothering them? Do they have a special toy or stuffed animal they confide in? What about a diary or journal?

The way characters in a book for young readers experience their emotions need to make sense to the reader first and foremost. This is a huge part of what makes characters relatable, and while you might feel ridiculous writing in a familiar blankie that provides nighttime Boogie Man Security and emotional support duty, there are plenty of children who will read that and feel less ridiculous for having their own blankies.

Early in this book, we talked about "building" a children's book. I encouraged you to ask yourself the following questions:

- What am I building?

- Who is going to use it?

- How should I build it?

As we reach the end of this book, you're likely aware that the last question isn't a simple one. How *should* you build your book?

Before reading this book, you might have said, "How do you write a children's book? Come up with a few subjects and verbs. Make sure they can understand the plot, so don't get too complicated. Don't use big words. Bam- done!"

Now you might say, "Well, every syllable of a children's book has a potential impact on their physical, mental, emotional, psychological, and artistic development, so just give up and don't bother."

Let's pump the brakes on the Failure Bus here—you *should* bother. We as humans love to bother with things that are tricky. We do crossword puzzles and jigsaw puzzles. We put together a bunch of foods to make complicated dishes. We paint, we draw, we tie knots and make usable clothing, and we spend hours staring at a screen, fine-tuning our reflexes so we can get to the next level in our favorite video game.

We don't write because it's easy.

We don't write because we expect everything we write to be an amazing world-wide success.

We don't write because we like fan mail and signing autographs.

We write because we love to write.

The best way to write is to write. That's why I've included so many exercises and examples throughout this book—because none of this comes easily. Have you noticed that every section of this book has ridden a "yes, but" or "yes, and" loop right around to previous sections? Have you grasped that a lot of the spinning plates rotate on the same spindles?

It may seem that you have a load of tricky problems to solve and gravely serious intricacies to keep in mind as you take on your first children's book, but if you try some of these exercises, come up with your own examples, do a little research in your target audience, and enjoy your practice sessions, you'll find that they all sort of loop into each other, like a hug. When your main character is relatable, they'll use words that make sense. They'll naturally explain and react to difficult concepts in a way that readers can understand. It's practice that makes all of these things possible.

Insight into Kids and Books : Inclusivity

More than anything—more than a billion, gajillion dollars and all the candy in the world—children want one thing: to be seen and understood. If we were being honest with ourselves as adults, we would agree. It's one thing to relate to a character based on what they do or say or how they feel, but it's an entirely separate thing for your character to know what it's like to be "different."

That word can mean a lot of different things, depending on your audience. They might have a different skin color than the other kids they know. They might have a different family structure than what they see in books and on TV. Maybe a child uses mobility devices, or glasses, or hearing aids. Perhaps they attend special classes at school, or need to take medicine to keep them feeling well.

I vividly remember the experience of getting glasses. I was in fifth grade. One day I was my happy, regular self, chatting with a friend as we headed down to the nurse's station for a vision check. A week later, I had a giant pair of glasses weighing down my growing nose and ears.

Not only were my glasses physically unfamiliar, but they were socially awkward. They fell off at the wrong times, and I kept accidentally touching them and smearing fingerprints across the lenses.

But my classmates were actually very excited about my glasses. I was the first one in the class to get glasses, so they all wanted to try them out. Everyone took turns using my glasses until the teacher reminded us all that they were mine because I needed them. By that time, however, I was already feeling like this particular difference wasn't really that big of a deal—just an inconvenience I would get used to.

As a newly-bespectacled child, I remember taking heart in knowing that I wasn't the first youngster to struggle with glasses. Arthur the aardvark wears glasses. John Bellairs' young awkward hero Johnny Dixon wears glasses. Even Harry Potter wears glasses. Providing children with a character who has the same differences can help them feel a lot more seen and a lot less alone in the literary world.

Adding characters who are also different, whether in appearance or ability, can be a great way to connect with your audience—but as with everything in a children's book, it's best to proceed with caution.

It's important to not only understand whatever situation is impacting your character's life, but to also understand how a child would interpret the situation. A young diabetic who has just been diagnosed is going to have a much simpler understanding of insulin and blood sugar than an adult who has grown up with Type 1 diabetes.

Therefore, I suggest you not only be clinical in your treatment of different abilities, appearances, and situations, but clinical from a child's perspective.

Thankfully, there are resources that will help you do just this. Support guides, websites, and informational pamphlets are offered to children who are experiencing all sorts of things in life that they possibly weren't prepared to handle, or weren't offered a choice in dealing with.

Using the appropriate terminology for not just the situation but for a child experiencing that situation can go miles in ensuring they aren't left feeling further ostracized by a character who should understand them... but just doesn't.

Conclusion

L et's look at those three questions one last time together:

- What am I building?

- Who is going to use it?

- How should I build it?

When you started this book, you might have assumed that I would give you the answers to each of these questions. Instead, I tried to provide you with guidance to help you answer each of these questions personally, individually, for each and every unique writing project you undertake.

I did this because there really isn't a formula. How many times did I provide examples of exceptions throughout the course of this book? And consider the number of times we tried exercises from different perspectives, age groups, and desired outcomes. There are so many moving pieces, all of which are quite delicate, and though I've assured you that they all come together, how do you really know that's true?

You know it's true because the proof is everywhere. You read and enjoyed books as a child. Children continue to read and enjoy books. It can be done!

To prove this to yourself, I encourage you to go read a bunch of children's books. Picture books, board books, A Child's Guide to Yosemite... whatever strikes your fancy. Choose things you want to read. Do the thing you're never supposed to do and grab books based exclusively on their covers.

Then, as you read them, think about all of the strange spirals and swirls of sometimes conflicting information you've encountered in this book. You'll start to see some of my examples come to life in each page you consume.

Then try it for yourself. Now that you know what a children's book looks like and feels like, try some of the exercises I've outlined here. Where I've given my own examples, try writing your own. And keep going. Always keep going and keep practicing, because I swear it gets more fun the more you do it.

How would I say I build a children's book? The first word that comes to mind is "delicately." Then "carefully." Then "effectively." We build a book to be something that a child needs, wants, and cherishes, of course, but most importantly, we are here to be an Agent of Discovery. We use our words to guide children through new places in the world, in their hearts, and in their imaginations. That's why I would say "delicately, carefully, and effectively" are the three main construction methods I use when building a book for a young reader.

But of course, I'm just the Agent of Discovery. What the reader does from here is entirely up to them...And maybe you. Go forth and create, and see how many doors you can open for young readers!

Bonus: Exercise Workbook

F or most writers, the hardest part is putting the words together to make a book. This seems somewhat obvious, but it's a little deeper than choosing the right word to describe a particular shade of red or the fluffiness of a dog.

Each word an author writes is a part of the whole book. Each word matters. When we're writing casually for other adults, we don't often actively consider this. Marketing and advertising specialists are actively aware of how words work on a psychological and emotional level, but most of us write with the intention of sharing information.

When we choose to write a book, we move beyond basic information sharing. This isn't an email to Payroll to advise of upcoming time off. This is an opportunity to reach out and touch the brains and hearts of readers. You can ignite emotions, reveal new information, and provide life-changing details all by arranging some words on a page.

And when you choose to write a book for children, the challenge is even greater. The stakes are higher, with an audience who needs greater engagement, and who may have never encountered the words with which you've written your book. Finding just the right words to grab their attention, to entertain them, to educate them, and to create a lasting memory in their lives? It seems impossible, but struggling through practice to get just the right message in front of just the right child is absolutely worth it.

1. Kimberly was late to Physics again, so Mr. Thompson was already glaring at her before she even sat down. It wasn't her fault that Aunt Flo had decided to show up a few days early. It also wasn't Kimberly's fault that the building designer hadn't put a bathroom in the Science wing of the high school building.

2. Eddie didn't know what to do. Every time he thought of his Pop-Pop, he wanted to cry. He would never see Pop-Pop again. This made him want to see Pop-Pop even more. But Pop-Pop wasn't here anymore.

3. Jim did not like Harry. Harry was mean. Harry pushed Jim by the swings. Jim fell. All the children laughed. Jim hurt his knee when he fell. Jim told Mrs. Dickinson. "Harry pushed me," he said. "Harry is a bully."

I also asked you to consider the following questions as you read each example:

- *What are your thoughts about each example?*

- *Who do you think each snippet was written for?*

- *What information do readers need to understand in order to empathize with the information provided?*

- *Can you think of a situation in which it would not be appropriate for a reader to come upon a passage like any of these?*

As you go forth with your daily reading and writing practices, I urge you to grab a passage that stands out to you– either from an article, story, social media post, or whatever speaks to you. Ask yourself those questions about that particular passage– and then rewrite each passage to simplify it.

At first, I recommend simplifying until you need absolutely every syllable to convey an idea. But as you continue practicing this exercise, you'll start to find areas where you can add a little extra something that magnifies your story without diminishing its simplicity. It's an extraordinary balancing act that truly requires practice!

Exercise: Practicing Descriptions

To begin this exercise, I prompted you to think about a specific animal: *How would you explain things like tentacles, beaks, talons, and hooves to someone who has no idea what those things look or feel like?*

I urged you to jot down some potential questions from someone learning about these things for the first time. Here is an extended version of that list:

- How would you explain the texture of different animals?

- What colors are they?

- What makes them distinctive from other animals?

- How do they move?

- What does it look like when they move?

- Are they fast or slow?

- What sounds do they make?

- How do they make those sounds?

- Under what circumstances do they make those sounds?

- How big or small are they?

- Do they have a certain smell?

These are just a few types of questions you can ask yourself as you're attempting to describe something to a brand-new audience. And while the original example in the chapter references animals, you can actually use these questions in regard to any tangible object.

In fact, the exercise encourages you to choose an object that you could observe every single day and in great detail since not all of us have tentacles, beaks, talons, or hooves at our beck and call. The example I provided was my poor, abused dish sponge, which is mercifully not yet sentient.

My dish sponge is:
- *Stinky*

- *Faded green*

- *Supposed to look like a sloth*

- *Hanging from a peg in my sink*

- *Has a soft side and a rough scrubby side*

- *Overdue for replacement*

From here, I encouraged you to put the terms together to create an accurate description. Using the concepts from the Simplify exercise, we considered which descriptors are really necessary to convey to the reader the true state of my dish sponge.

I decided upon:

My dish sponge is light green. It's stinky because I use it every single day. One side of the sponge is soft like a towel. The other side is rough and scratchy. I use that side to help scrape off food that gets stuck to my dishes.

But as the chapter continues to explain, descriptions are not a one-size-fits-all experience. There are many ways to describe anything, and it is up to you as a writer to determine which details are important, and which are less essential.

Sometimes providing the description your reader wants and needs is as simple as asking yourself what you want and need your reader to know. By practicing descriptions, you can find your stride and the right level of description to take your reader on a "just-right" journey.

Exercise: How We Got There

First, you find or write a single sentence:

Waldo ate eggs for breakfast on Wednesday morning.

Then you write another sentence that doesn't seem to relate at first:

Waldo was happy to have new tap dancing shoes today.

From here, you just need to fill in the details to make an entire story:

Waldo ate eggs for breakfast on Wednesday morning. He was nervous, because he had dance class that afternoon. His class was learning a new tap dance. Last week, Waldo's tap shoe had broken during class, and he slipped and fell. Waldo was happy to have new tap dancing shoes today, but still a little nervous. What if the other kids made fun of him about his fall?

The idea behind this exercise is that you really can get from one idea to another through infinite paths; however, not every path will be ideal for your book. When you're working on a draft, you will likely have a good idea of where you are and where you want to be as the pages progress, but as anyone who has taken a family hiking will tell you, choosing the path that is equal parts educational, easy to navigate, and scenic is often harder than the physical activity itself.

Try different paths between the first and second sentences. I could've gone in an entirely different direction:

Waldo ate eggs for breakfast on Wednesday morning. It was his first time eating duck eggs, and he found them very delicious and rich, just like his new friend Wendy had told them they would be.

Wendy was his partner in tap dancing class. She lived on a farm, and sometimes she brought tasty things in for the class to try, like these duck eggs. She also told him that his old, sweaty tap dancing shoes were gross and that if he came to class with new shoes, she would give him an entire loaf of homemade pumpkin bread made from pumpkins she had actually grown herself.

Waldo was happy to have new tap dancing shoes today.

I honestly adore this exercise, because it can go anywhere. In high school, I would find my first sentence in a serious newspaper and the second in a celebrity gossip rag, just to make things interesting– hence my suggestion to borrow sentences if you don't happen to have your own handy. This isn't about being lazy and unable to come up with original content- it's about being able to jump in and write even when you aren't entirely sure what's happening. The bigger the disparity between sources, the harder you'll work to close the gap.

Exercise: Narrate Your Day... For Kids

This exercise is a favorite warmup of mine, as I can just refocus my attention on what I'm doing as if I were writing a scene in a new book:

"She continued typing the sentence, occasionally striking the wrong key, cursing and pausing to sip her apple-honey tea before correcting the error. It was no wonder she kept losing her train of thought, she chided herself. Still, the tea was delicious, the local honey supported farmers in her community, and she reminded herself that hydration and small treats are important for your overall health."

Then I encouraged you to flip the lens to that of a child. What do you think a child would want to get out of your narration? What were the important events and details?

The example I came up with was:

"She kept typing and typing. Every now and then something went wrong. It was easy to tell because she would stop typing and loudly say some adult words. Then she would take a sip of tea and start typing again like nothing had happened."

But as you may recall, I didn't like that, so I switched it up again:

"She drank a lot of tea. She said it kept her calm, but the only time she drank it was when she made a mistake in her typing. Then she yelled bad words and drank a lot of tea."

Granted, this exercise shares a lot in common with Simplify and Practicing Descriptions. In this context, however, we're focusing on connecting with your Inner Children's Narrator.

When you narrate your day under normal circumstances, you're likely doing so as an adult, about your adult world, in adult terms. Changing this exercise to consider how a child would narrate your day can help you feel more natural and confident when writing narratives for children.

Finding your voice is the best way to get cozy in your role as a children's author. Exercises like this will help you figure out exactly who you are and how you sound when you're using literature to "speak."

Exercise: Dear Journal

Generally speaking, completing this exercise should be a lot less interesting or introspective than therapeutic journaling. To get started, I recommend focusing on actual events and observable situations. Start with the verbs or the most obvious things that come to mind.

In my example, I narrated my morning in the first person:

I woke up with a big, fluffy kitty on my chest. The world was dark on the other side of my bedroom curtains. I wished that Polly's breakfast time and my sleeping schedule were the same, just once.

After making Polly's wishes come true, showering, and brushing my teeth, it seemed like a good idea to get the day started. I plopped down into my rolling desk chair, causing it to scoot just far enough away from my desk that I couldn't reach the keyboard. "Great," I thought to myself. "It's going to be that kind of day."

As I stated, it's not dissimilar to journaling but with the intention of writing for an audience. If I were to journal a morning like this, it would probably include more colorful language and be indicative of childhood trauma.

Writing a book for children includes a strong element of storytelling, even if the story is quite true. Just as Narrate Your Day is intended to be entertaining, so too is Dear Journal.

If you are looking to practice first-person narrative, Dear Journal can help you get started. Quite honestly, when I'm actively working on a book, I do these exercises as the narrator of that book.

In fact, if it's a fiction piece, I might perform this exercise from the point of view of the main character. Perhaps Ralph the friendly neighborhood mechanic woke up with a huge cramp in his left foot. He then ate a banana, which helped a lot. He couldn't get back to sleep, so he cruised some online engine-rebuilding forums. That's just the kind of guy he is, and if Ralph the friendly mechanic is the main character of my book, I should really know what kind of guy he is.

And if I don't like what comes out of that, I adjust it. That's why this is practice; this is why these are exercises.

Exercise: Make It Interesting, Not Longer

Brevity is the soul of wit, but it takes a lot more words than that to explain what that sentence even means to a small child. In this exercise, we work on coloring between the lines from a literary perspective.

In my example, I attempted to write a short biography about Fred Rogers.

Fred Rogers used his imagination to create a world known as Mr. Rogers' Neighborhood. This world became a television show. On his show, Mr. Rogers used puppets and songs to teach children about the world around them.

All of that is true, but it's also boring, as I noted. So I tried a more emotional and sincere approach to my homage:

With the ding of a trolley bell and a song that everyone knew, children were able to visit Mr. Rogers' Neighborhood for 33 years thanks to television. Fred Rogers was a trained musician who made up songs and skits for his puppet characters. He liked to talk about things like feelings and dealing with problems.

This version, however, is a whopping 18 words longer than the first. Ergo, I endeavored to be short and sweet:

Thanks to public television, children could hop aboard the Neighborhood Trolley and visit Mr. Roger's Neighborhood. Fred Rogers was a trained musician who made up songs and skits for his puppet characters. He liked to talk about things like feelings and dealing with problems.

This version is still longer than the original but perhaps captures more of the essence of who Mr. Rogers really was.

In fact, I'm still not satisfied with this explanation. Perhaps:

For several decades, children around the United States knew that a man wearing a fuzzy button-down sweater was proud of them. Mr. Fred Rogers was a musician who shared a very special imaginary world where it was ok to talk about feelings and problems.

This is quite honestly the point, though. You keep going at these exercises until you either resign yourself to throwing your writing implements off a cliff, or you realize with a sudden bolt of pride that you have written the most perfect version of your ideas. Then you stop and do it again tomorrow.

5 Writing Exercises

If you're interested in learning to write books, chances are high that you've tried before and gotten stuck. As a result, you may be even less enthusiastic about trying again. If that's the case, check out some personally selected writing exercises from author Lauren Bingham's vault of helpful tricks and tips for getting the cursor moving again... or for the first time.

Go to https://subscribepage.io/5-Writing-Exercises

to download your own copy of Lauren Bingham's Five Favorite Writing Exercises.

About the Author

Lauren Bingham grew up in a house full of books. A dedicated bibliophile by first grade, she often got into trouble for voraciously consuming any written material—from consuming Reader's Digest cover to cover in one sitting to completing library books before they even made it home.

Lauren has been avidly writing for pure passion since childhood, and thanks to the internet for providing a comfortable place where all writers are welcome. Ghostwriting and copywriting since the early 2000s, she believes strongly that there is a story in each of us and that any time is a great time to share those stories with others.

If you're interested in learning to write books, chances are high that you've tried before and gotten stuck. As a result, you may be even less enthusiastic about trying again. If that's the case, check out some personally selected writing exercises from author Lauren Bingham's vault of helpful tricks and tips for getting the cursor moving again... or for the first time.

Reviews and feedback help improve this book and the author. If you enjoy this book, we would greatly appreciate it if you could take a few moments to share your opinion and post a review on Amazon. Thank you!

Also by Lauren Bingham